GUN CONTROL

GUN CONTROL

A Decision for Americans

by Edward F. Dolan, Jr.

A GROLIER COMPANY

FRANKLIN WATTS
NEW YORK/LONDON/TORONTO/SYDNEY/1982
AN IMPACT BOOK/REVISED EDITION

52378

Library of Congress Cataloging in Publication Data

DOLAN, Edward F   1924—
Gun control.

(An Impact book)
Bibliography: p.
Includes index.
SUMMARY: Discusses both sides of the
gun control debate including the use of firearms
in the United States historically and at present and
existing gun control laws both here and abroad.
1. Firearms — Laws and regulations —
United States — Juvenile literature.
2. Firearms — Laws and regulations —
Juvenile literature. [1. Firearms —
Laws and regulations] I. Title.
KF3941.Z9D64   344'.73'0533   78-5576
ISBN 0—531—02202—1

51068

84- 14874

I am indebted to many people for their help in the preparation of this book. Special thanks must go to Richard B. Lyttle and William Royse, both of Marin County, California, for their editorial comments and suggestions; to Tacy Cook for her review of the manuscript for accuracy; and to Congressman Steve Symms of Idaho, the Bureau of Alcohol, Tobacco and Firearms of the Department of the Treasury, the National Council to Control Handguns (and especially Charles Orasin and Melanie Woolston), the National Gun Control Center, the National Rifle Association, and the United States Conference of Mayors.

An extra word of thanks is due the National Council to Control Handguns to reprint the charts from its booklet, *The Case To Control Handguns* on pages 11, 54, 57, 62 and 75.

Contents

This book is for my brother Michael

GUN CONTROL

Introduction

Americans participated in a great debate throughout the 1960s and 1970s. The debate continues into the 1980s. It is the argument over whether the use of the 150 million handguns, shotguns, and rifles in the United States should be restricted or banned altogether. And if so, how?

Opinions on what should be done conflict sharply. Many Americans are confused by all that has been said.

On the one hand, we hear that something must be done immediately to stop the havoc wrought by the gun. Statistics tell us that it is responsible for more than 30,000 murders, suicides, and accidental deaths each year. It is used in countless crimes and is said either to breed or reflect the violence that has become such a significant and frightening aspect of our national life.

During the past two decades, the gun has been leveled against some of our most revered political and social leaders. It has cut down John F. Kennedy, Robert F. Kennedy, and Martin Luther King. It has left a fourth, Governor George Wallace of Alabama, crippled for life. Twice in the 1970s, it was used in an attempt to assassinate President Gerald Ford.

Violent crimes involving the gun have also scarred the opening years of the 1980s. On the night of December 8, 1980, singer John Lennon was murdered by a gunman as he and his wife were entering the courtyard of their New York City apartment. A little more than three months later, newly-elected President Ronald Reagan became the victim of a wound from a small-caliber revolver held in the hands of a would-be assassin. In a two-second burst of gunfire, the President and his surrounding aides were injured. Miraculously, no one was killed.

All the victims mentioned above were well known public figures. But guns have also taken the lives of countless men and women who were not famous and who were known only to their friends and loved ones. As you will see in the opening chapters of this book, more than 20,000 Americans are murdered each year. Guns of all types — rifles, shotguns, and handguns — are responsible for approximately 66 percent of these deaths. By itself, the handgun is responsible for more than 10,000 deaths.

Dead because of gunshot wounds are Americans from all walks of life. Look at what happened in Washington, D.C., during the first eight days of December 1980:

- December 3 — An argument broke out between two young men. A gun was fired. Dead was a twenty-year-old man.
- December 3 — Another argument broke out, this time on a playground. There were gunshots. A nineteen-year-old youth fell wounded. He died five days later.
- December 5 — A nationally known physician, Dr. Michael Halberstam, died of gunshot wounds when he surprised a burglar in his home.
- December 6 — A fifteen-year-old boy was killed when a fight at a gasoline station led to shots being fired.

- December 6 — A man in his twenties was shot and killed as he attempted to rob a dry cleaning store.
- December 8 — A thirty-year-old florist took the receipts from his shop to the bank for deposit. A robbery was attempted while he was there. The florist always armed himself with a gun for protection when carrying a large amount in receipts. He died of bullet wounds suffered in an exchange of shots with the robber.

And so, with an increasing number of lives being taken each year, there is a call to control the gun, to curtail its use and the ease with which it may be purchased in many parts of the country, or to be rid of it altogether. But this is only one side of the debate. On the other hand, we hear the arguments of many responsible Americans who, despite the appalling death rate, feel that we have the right to own firearms.

Opponents of strict gun controls argue that the right to own firearms is guaranteed by the Constitution. The claim is made that, without firearms, we would be more vulnerable than ever to criminal violence. Moreover, they claim, we would be unable to defend ourselves if subversive elements, a would-be dictator, or some foreign intruder attempted to take hold of the country. The privately owned gun helped us to win our freedom in the first place, they say; it can help us preserve that freedom today.

Further, the opponents of gun control tell us that gun-control laws don't work because the people who cause most of the trouble — the criminals — simply won't bother to obey them. But the proponents of control reply by producing statistics to show that control laws have kept the crime rates down in other nations. Strictly enforced controls, they believe, can do the same thing here.

Basically, the anti-control people feel that to call for

and enact laws against the gun is to move in the wrong direction. They recognize that there is much violence in our society and know that something must be done about it. But they argue that when the gun is involved in violence, it is not, in itself, responsible for the trouble. A gun, after all, is an inanimate object that is incapable of acting on its own. The fault lies with the people who misuse it — the criminals, the mentally ill, the emotionally unstable, the intoxicated. It will do no good, then, to move against the gun. Violence will be reduced only if we restrict the people who pull the trigger.

These various pro-and-con arguments — and the myriad others that are linked to them — seem to have much substance when presented quietly and reasonably.

And so, as an average American listening to all that is being said, what are you to do? Should you be for or against gun control? As is usual in any public debate, you have to make up your own mind.

The purpose of this book is to help you do so. We'll look at all aspects of the debate and the circumstances that gave birth to it. We'll start with the widespread use of firearms in the United States and discuss the damage it does. Then we'll turn to what is called "the tradition of the gun" in America, glancing back through the years to see the part that firearms played in our history. From there, we'll move to existing gun-control laws, and then spend several chapters on both sides of the debate. Afterward, we'll discuss how existing laws here and abroad work. Finally, there will be an up-to-date report on what is happening today in this country's efforts to solve the gun problem. We'll look at the newest laws on gun control that are being proposed for study by Congress.

One point must be made right at the outset. In the coming pages, you're going to read much about the violence in the United States. It's a violence that disgusts sensitive Americans everywhere (just as it undoubtedly disgusts you) and it has caused many of them to become disgusted with the country itself.

The violence deserves our disgust. But the disgust of country because of it is undeserved and prompts us to forget the many healthy, enjoyable, and fruitful aspects of life here. It should also be remembered that violence is not a problem found only in the United States. In this troubled twentieth century, it is a worldwide problem. Look at almost any newspaper headline on almost any day of the week. You will read about violence and turmoil in many countries. There has been violent fighting in northern Ireland for years. Just recently, the world witnessed the shooting and wounding of the Pope in Italy. In Egypt, President Anwar Sadat was assassinated. In Great Britain, there have been racial difficulties that have resulted in rioting. Political figures in France and Italy have been attacked or kidnapped. Accounts of the torture of political prisoners have reached us from South America and Southeast Asia. And in Iran, an attack on the American embassy led to more than fifty of our people being held captive for more than a year.

The problem of violence, then, is not ours alone. But Americans do have to face one fact — to a great degree, violence in the United States is different from that found elsewhere. Most violence abroad can be traced to political roots. Some of the violence in our country is politically motivated, too. But, far more than in other countries, our violence springs from criminal activities and personal disputes.

There is no doubt that the gun plays a role in the violence in America, whether political, criminal, or personal in nature. But what can be done to solve matters? Should the gun be controlled? If so, to what degree? Will controls actually do any good? Or will they deprive us of certain rights? Should we take harsher action against the people who misuse the gun instead of trying to control the gun itself?

Hopefully, this book will help you find your own answers to these questions and will enable you to reach an informed decision on gun control in the United States. With your decision firmly in hand, you may be able to contribute to the debate and to its successful conclusion.

Yours is a decision that all Americans must soon reach.

Chapter One
AN ARMED CAMP

"I'd say that the United States
is an armed camp."

These words came from an English visitor a few months ago when I told him of some of the statistics I was collecting for this book.

Like most Americans, I don't enjoy hearing someone from abroad criticize my country. I wanted to argue with him, but I had to admit that the figures were pretty startling. At present, an estimated 150 million firearms of all types — rifles, shotguns, pistols, and revolvers — are to be found in the United States. They outnumber all our cars, trucks, and buses by more than 25 million. About one-half the nation's families have a gun of some sort in the house.

I was able to say, though, that millions of these guns are kept by law-abiding citizens for the lawful protection of their homes and will probably never be fired. And that millions more are owned by responsible sportsmen for hunting, trapshooting, and target shooting.

But my friend just shook his head. "One hundred

and fifty million guns. It doesn't matter what they're used for. If they're all loaded, someone's bound to get hurt."

I had no answer. He was right. To know just how right, you need only look in a newspaper almost any day of the week.

For instance, if you live in the San Francisco area, you may have read of the death of an elderly shopkeeper in a recent armed robbery. Robbed twice before, he kept a pistol hidden near his cash register. He pulled the gun out and died an instant later when one of the robbers shot him in the chest. His assailant was a seventeen-year-old boy.

If your home is in Pennsylvania, you may have read of the child who found a .45 caliber revolver while playing in his parents' bedroom. He toyed with the gun for a moment. Then he pressed the trigger. The child was dead at four years of age.

Or, if you live in or near Chicago, perhaps you'll never forget the tragedy of the thirteen-year-old boy who first lost his mother to cancer. Then his sister was crippled for life when, examining a gun in her father's weapons collection, she accidentally discharged it. Next, the despondent father took a gun from the collection and committed suicide with it. Unable to bear all that had happened to his family, the boy also went to the collection, selected a gun, and ended his life.

A Federal Bureau of Investigation study, which was made in 1980, shows that an estimated 21,860 Americans are now murdered annually; 62 percent of the killings are done with firearms. Each year, more than 10,000 people use a gun to commit suicide; in 1977 alone, 16,084 people took their lives with guns and explosives; of those deaths, 90 percent were caused by all types of firearms, and 50 percent by handguns alone. Close to 2,000 citizens die in gun accidents annually, with the number being 1,806 in 1980. Another 200,000 are injured.

(8)

The havoc wrought by firearms is perhaps most dramatically seen in one fact alone. During the peak years of the Vietnam War (1966–1972), the United States lost 43,000 men killed in combat. It was a death figure that aroused the entire nation. But, in those same seven years, we saw a far greater number of American civilians murdered with firearms. Murders with guns took 71,804 lives between 1966 and 1972.

Indeed, as my friend said, America does seem to be an armed camp — with terrible results for thousands of its citizens each year.

THE MOST DANGEROUS GUN

While all firearms are dangerous, I told my friend that revolvers and pistols loom as the most dangerous of all. Known as handguns, they are involved in the majority of U.S. crimes, suicides, and accidents. Rifles and shotguns, on the other hand, are mostly used for legitimate purposes by America's 20 million sportsmen and play only a small role in crime.

For instance, though all types of firearms account for 62 percent of the nation's annual murders, the rifle is responsible for only 5 percent of the killings, and the shotgun for 7 percent. These long guns, as they are called, trail well behind the knife, which is to blame 19 percent of the time. They run a little behind clubs and poison (13 percent) and are about even with assault with the hands and feet (6 percent). But the handgun is responsible for 50 percent of our murders.

In actual figures, the handgun kills approximately 10,980 of the 21,860 Americans murdered annually. These deaths break down to about thirty a day. When you add handgun suicides and fatal accidents to the list, the daily toll rises to over sixty — or just under three deaths every hour.

(9)

Further, the handgun is used each year in about 150,000 armed robberies and in more than 100,000 aggravated assaults. Attorney General Edward Levi told the Senate Juvenile Delinquency Committee in 1975 that the handgun puts in an appearance in one out of every three armed robberies and in one out of every four aggravated assaults.

No one knows exactly how many handguns are to be found in the nation. But some recent figures can give us a pretty good idea. The U.S. Bureau of Alcohol, Tobacco and Firearms reports that some 40 million handguns were owned by Americans in 1974. In each year since 1972, the United States has manufactured at least 1.5 million handguns while importing another 400,000 to 1 million — for an annual total of between 2 and 2.5 million new weapons. And so today's grand total is set at about fifty-six million, meaning one handgun to every four or five citizens.

It is said today a new handgun is sold every thirteen seconds in the United States. If handguns continue to be manufactured and purchased at their present rate, there will be 100 million of them in the country by the year 2000.

The figure alarms many Americans. Their alarm grows when they look at what happened to the nation's murder rate between 1964 and 1974, a period that saw our people buy more firearms than ever before. (We'll see the reasons for this buying boom in later chapters.) In 1964, fewer than 28 million handguns were owned by Americans. By 1974, the total was up to 40 million. In the years between, the nation's overall murder rate doubled. The murder rate by handguns nearly tripled itself.

What will the murder rate be, concerned Americans ask, when there are 100 million handguns in the country — at least double the number that are here now?

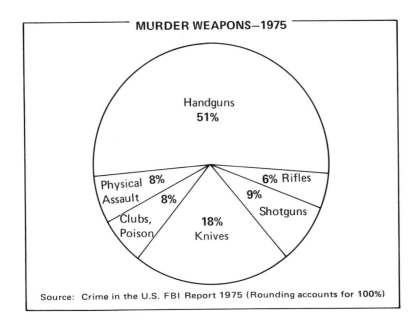

MURDER WEAPONS—1975

Handguns
51%

Physical 8%
Assault

8%

Clubs,
Poison

18%
Knives

6% Rifles

9%

Shotguns

Source: Crime in the U.S. FBI Report 1975 (Rounding accounts for 100%)

TWO QUESTIONS

The widespread ownership of guns in the United States shocks my English friend. It is a feeling he shares with people in many other countries.

He believes that he has a right to be shocked. His own people have always disliked guns and have controlled their ownership for years. He says the results have been happy ones. The city of London reported only two handgun murders in 1972. There were forty-three in Boston that same year. London's population is twelve times greater than Boston's.

Japan is another country that controls gun ownership. In 1971, just one person was murdered by a handgun in Tokyo. But there were 308 handgun killings in Los Angeles County. Tokyo has a population of 11 million. Los Angeles County's is 7 million.

These are not just isolated examples. The fact is that the American death toll from all kinds of guns — and from

(11)

the handgun in particular — leads those of all other nations by a wide margin.

My friend is not only shocked but bewildered. It seems obvious to him that the laws controlling gun ownership have kept the murder rates low in England and Japan. And so he asked me two questions:

"Why do you allow so many guns in your country? Why doesn't the United States do something to control their use?"

The questions aren't the easiest in the world to answer. The first brings us to a long-standing American tradition and to some dangers that many of our people see in our society today. The second has prompted a great debate in the United States, an argument that has been raging since the 1960s and that may continue to rage for years to come.

There is no doubt that America's gun problem is a great and dangerous one. The statistics of the harm done speak for themselves. And so it may seem strange that there should be any argument at all about solving it. But there is, with the people on both sides recognizing the problem but having opposing views on its solution. Their debate is not over *whether* the problem should be solved but *how*.

On one side of the fence are people who believe that the ownership of guns should be restricted or banned altogether by federal law. On the other side are those who predict that gun-control laws will do no good, that they won't be obeyed by the country's criminal element, and that they will deprive Americans of certain basic rights and leave us unable to defend ourselves against the attacks of criminals, foreign invaders, or — should that terrible day ever come — a dictatorial government in Washington, D.C.

My friend's two questions stand at the heart of this book. Let's look at each in turn.

Chapter Two

A MATTER OF TRADITION

"Why do you allow so many
guns in your country?"

I told my friend that the private ownership of firearms in the United States is a deeply rooted tradition. Actually, two traditions surround the gun. One is historical and the other romantic.

THE HISTORICAL TRADITION

It goes without saying that the privately owned gun has been a part of the American scene since the earliest days of our history. For the first settlers here, it was as necessary as food, clothing, and shelter. They were people who were challenging a hostile wilderness. The gun was a must for hunting and protection.

Later, the privately owned gun played a major — if not a decisive — role in the winning of our independence as a nation. Historians have often said that, without the old flintlock that hung on the kitchen door or above the fireplace mantel, the colonists could never have gone out to meet the British at Lexington. Then, throughout the

(13)

years of fighting that followed, the Continental Army was practically always penniless and poorly equipped. Had not the American soldiers brought their own muskets from home, there likely wouldn't have been enough weapons to go around.

Once our independence was won, the gun found a place in U.S. law. It was mentioned in the second of the original ten amendments to the Constitution. The amendment takes but a few words:

"A well regulated militia being necessary to the security of a free State, the right of the people to keep and bear arms shall not be infringed."

The Founding Fathers were thinking of three things when they wrote the amendment. First, they remembered what it was like to be under the thumb of the British, and they wanted to protect the people should the United States itself ever produce an oppressive government. Second, they knew that their infant country was weak and prone to attack from foreign nations that had no wish to see it grow strong or even survive. Finally, they did not wish— nor could they afford—to mount a giant national army.

And so the best defense against oppression from within or attack from without seemed to be state militias. They would be small amateur armies made up of citizens who, grabbing up guns from home, could spring quickly into action.

Two of our finest early leaders agreed with this approach. Thomas Jefferson, when drafting the Virginia Constitution, wrote, "No freeman will ever be disbarred the use of arms." And George Washington believed that "a free people ought not only be armed and disciplined" but should manufacture their own weapons and military supplies so that they need never depend on someone else for them.

From the Eastern seaboard, the privately owned gun moved deeper and deeper into the frontier. Carried in a holster, propped against the driver's seat of a Conestoga wagon, or slung across a saddle, it played a vital role in the opening of the West. By the dawn of our century, when the country was settled from coast to coast, the tradition that the American needed and had the right to own a gun was firmly rooted. It is still with us today, with a great many of our people keeping a firearm for the protection of their families, their homes, and their communities and for a variety of recreational purposes.

THE ROMANTIC TRADITION

The outlaw, his face dark with two days' growth of beard, stands in the blazing sunlight. He stares far along the dusty street to the town marshal. The marshal is tall and lean. His eyes are steady. He waits as townspeople run for shelter. He knows that frightened citizens are watching from windows and doorways. A woman in a poke bonnet dashes after a little boy who has wandered into the street and pulls him into an alleyway.

Now all is deathly quiet. The two men begin to walk slowly toward each other. Their hands are held stiffly out from their sides, their fingers spread and ready. Their eyes never waver. Suddenly, the outlaw's hand moves to the holster low on his hip.

But the marshal is faster. Guns roar, shattering the noon quiet. The marshal stands with a Colt .45 in his hand. The outlaw lies sprawled in the dust . . .

How often has this scene been played out in motion pictures or on television? How often has it been written in adventure stories? So often that it's impossible to really know.

But every American knows the scene itself. We've all encountered it time and again since earliest childhood. It's a classic scene that best represents the second tradition to grow up around the gun — the romantic tradition of the gun as a symbol of adventure and courage, and the instrument of right and justice.

(15)

The tradition was born in the second half of the nineteenth century when a group of cheaply printed magazines first went on sale. They were filled with exciting stories (said at the time to be true, but now known to be the wildest fiction) about such frontiersmen as Buffalo Bill Cody, Wyatt Earp, Bat Masterson, and Wild Bill Hickok. Read by countless people, young and old alike, who had little or no adventure in their own daily lives, these magazines soon became the most popular literature of the day in the eastern United States. Out of their pages stepped a new American folk hero — the Westerner.

He had all those traits that we Americans like. He was independent-minded. He was fearless. Strong. Determined. And, above all, he was a man of action, a man who overcame danger, righted wrongs, and brought the law to a wild frontier.

But he did these things with a six-gun. Soon, in the minds of people everywhere, the gun was as noble and as American as he, as much of a national tradition as he had become.

He and his holstered Colts have remained with us ever since, in the magazines, comic strips, and books of our own century. And especially in the Western motion picture, which began in 1903 with *The Great Train Robbery* and has gone on through the years to give us such gun-toting heroes as Tom Mix, Hoot Gibson, Tim McCoy, Gary Cooper, and the greatest of the lot, John Wayne. And let's not forget how radio and then television adopted the Western and made household names of the Lone Ranger, the Cisco Kid, and Dodge City's Marshal Matt Dillon.

But the Westerner, though he is the one most loved, is not the only American hero. His counterparts, all of them carrying guns, are to be seen everywhere in our literature, motion pictures, and television. There are private detectives Sam Spade, Cannon, and Barnaby Jones. There are the police department's Baretta, Pepper Anderson, and

Starsky and Hutch. There is the government's Lou Erskine of the FBI, and special agent Eliott Ness and his Untouchables. And there are the anti-heroes, the victims of society who fight back or get what they want with the gun — the Bonnies and Clydes of this world.

Many Americans feel that the romantic tradition has done terrible damage to the country's life. They say that it has linked a deadly weapon to the ideas of courage and strength. It has convinced too many people that they can take what they want, solve their problems, or ease their frustrations with a gun. And, by showing us one killing after another on the television and motion picture screen, it has so blunted our sensibilities that great segments of the public no longer fully comprehend the horror of violent death. All too easily someone can pick up a gun and fire it without actually realizing that he is not playacting, without actually understanding that, in the next instant, real and not make-believe blood is going to flow.

Those who deplore the tradition believe that the young American has been the one most damaged by it. He is raised around the gun. It is so commonplace and so often used that he forgets just how lethal it can be. The consequences can ruin — or take — his life.

THE TRADITIONS TOGETHER

To people who think as these Americans do, the situation becomes intolerable when the two traditions are joined. The first, establishing the idea that it is a basic American right to own a firearm, has put too many guns in private ownership and has made them too accessible. The second has made it all too easy for anyone to pick up the accessible gun in a moment of need, bravado, or anger.

Violence cannot help but follow.

Seeing these things, many Americans long ago began to ask the second question that my friend asked.

Chapter Three
ON THE BOOKS

"Why doesn't the United States
do something
to control the use of guns?"

Because we Americans own so many guns and because we're now arguing over how to control them, my friend had the impression that the United States has never done anything before about regulating the use of firearms.

Nothing could be further from the truth. I explained that the debate has been triggered not because we don't have any regulatory laws to begin with, but because, thanks to the growing violence in the nation, stronger controls than we've ever known are being sought. Throughout this century, a host of control measures have been put into effect in the country — at the city, county, state, and federal levels.

Just what are the laws we've passed?

STATE AND LOCAL LAWS

State and local laws cover all aspects of control — from the issuance of gun permits to regulations on whether a person may or may not carry a handgun concealed on his person or in his car.

But they're difficult to talk about. For one thing, there are too many of them for a book of this size to discuss in detail. Each state has developed its own set of laws, meaning fifty sets in all. As for local laws, it's estimated that they number around twenty thousand.

Matters are made even more difficult by the fact that the laws vary so much across the country. For instance, when you buy a gun in some states, you must wait a certain time — often five to ten days — before you can take it home. The waiting period enables the authorities to check your background to see if there's any reason why you shouldn't have the gun. But in other states, no waiting period is required.

To get an idea of the laws themselves and just how much they vary, let's start at the local level with four cities.

Suppose that you live in Atlanta, Georgia, or Denver, Colorado. You may purchase a handgun without a permit. But you'll be required to get a permit from the police department if you live in Detroit, Michigan. And, should you move to Washington, D.C., you won't be able to buy a new handgun at all. A recently enacted law forbids the purchase of handguns and allows you to own one only if it was in your possession at the time the law became effective. You must then register your gun with the police every year.

There are also variations to be found between the laws of a state and those of its cities. Louisiana state law does not require that a citizen have a permit to buy a gun. But, if your home is in the City of New Orleans, you'll have to go to the police department and obtain a permit. Then you'll have to show it to the store salesman before he can sell you the gun.

Let's stop in Missouri next, where the situation is somewhat reversed. In Kansas City, you'll find no specific permit requirements for gun ownership. But state law says that firearms that can be concealed on your person can only be bought with a permit which may be obtained from the local sheriff's office for a fee of fifty cents.

The quickest way to see how the state laws themselves vary is to run through the following chart. It was prepared by the U.S. Conference of Mayors and comes from their booklet, *Handgun Control . . . Issues and Alternatives*. The chart shows that:

ONLY IN THE FOLLOWING STATES
DO YOU NEED A PERMIT (OR SOMETHING
EQUIVALENT) TO PURCHASE A HANDGUN:

Hawaii	New Jersey
Massachusetts	New York
Michigan	North Carolina
Missouri	Virginia (certain counties)

(Ed. note: Illinois requires an
I.D. card issued by the state.)

IN THE FOLLOWING STATES,
YOU NEED A LICENSE TO CARRY A HANDGUN
ON OR ABOUT YOUR PERSON:

Concealed Only

Alabama	Nevada
California	New Hampshire (if
Colorado	gun is loaded)
Delaware	Oregon
Idaho	Pennsylvania
Iowa	South Dakota
Maine	Utah
Michigan	Virginia
Montana	Washington
Wyoming	

Concealed or Openly

Connecticut	Maryland
Florida	Massachusetts
Georgia	New Jersey
(openly only; con-	New York
cealed prohibited)	North Dakota
Hawaii	West Virginia
Indiana	District of Columbia

IN THE FOLLOWING STATES,
YOU MAY NOT CARRY A HANDGUN
ON YOUR PERSON AT ALL:

Concealed

Alaska	Mississippi
Arizona	Missouri
Illinois	Nebraska
Kansas	New Mexico (loaded)
Kentucky	North Carolina
Louisiana	Oklahoma
Wisconsin	

. . . . . MAY NOT CARRY A HANDGUN
ON YOUR PERSON AT ALL (cont.)

Concealed or Openly

Arkansas   Tennessee (with intent
(as a weapon) to go armed)
South Carolina Texas

IN THE FOLLOWING STATES,
YOU NEED A LICENSE TO CARRY A
HANDGUN IN A VEHICLE:

Concealed

California Idaho
Oregon

Concealed or Openly

Alabama   New Hampshire (loaded)
Connecticut   New Jersey
Hawaii   New York
Indiana   North Dakota
Iowa   Pennsylvania
Maryland   Rhode Island
Massachusetts South Dakota
Michigan   Washington (loaded)

IN THE FOLLOWING STATES, THERE
IS A WAITING PERIOD BETWEEN THE TIME
YOU PURCHASE A HANDGUN AND PICK IT UP:

Alabama   New Jersey
California   Oregon
Connecticut Pennsylvania
Illinois   Rhode Island
Indiana   South Dakota
Maryland   Tennessee
Washington

Though the state laws vary, there is at least one major point on which practically all agree. It can be seen in the above laws: they're all directed against the handgun. To stress again what was said in chapter one, the handgun is the most dangerous weapon of all so far as crime and bodily injury are concerned, and the states recognize this fact. Along with the federal government, they look on rifles and shotguns as relatively harmless, used mostly as they are for sporting purposes.

As will be seen later, the many and varied state and local laws are a source of worry to the people who advocate gun control. The welter of laws, they argue, makes it all but impossible to regulate the use of firearms in an orderly fashion all across the country. What's needed instead is a broad federal law that will apply wherever a gun is purchased in the United States.

The federal laws that have been enacted are few in number and so are much easier to talk about.

FEDERAL LAWS

The first federal laws were passed in the early 1900s and dealt with both firearms and explosives. Actually, they were mostly concerned with explosives. Their chief aim was to set up safety standards for the manufacture, shipment, and use of black powder, dynamite, and TNT, which were all needed for construction and mining work. The laws were also intended to keep explosives from being used for criminal purposes.

In the late 1920s, however, federal attention shifted to the firearm. These were the years of Prohibition, when liquor could not be legally made and sold in the United States. Many of our cities watched, appalled, as gangsters fought it out to see who would win control of the rich trade in illegal liquor. Their gun battles created an

(24)

atmosphere that triggered criminal activities of all types throughout the nation.

Seen for the first time in all its danger by an alarmed public was the handgun. Hoodlums of every type could easily carry it concealed in their clothes, ready for instant use. They could just as easily pass it or mail it from one to another. Unlike long guns and machine guns, it could be mailed in the smallest and most innocent looking of packages.

And so, in 1927, Congress moved against the handgun by passing the Mailing of Firearms Act. The act was a simple one. It prohibited all but certain people from sending a "concealable" weapon — a pistol or revolver — through the mails. The people exempted from the act included the police and the military, and arms manufacturers and dealers when engaged in legitimate business.

Six years later — on June 26, 1934 — another federal gun-control law passed in Congress. Called the National Firearms Act, it was aimed at cutting down on the manufacture of the weapons most used by criminals. Manufacturers were required to pay a heavy tax and to register themselves with the government when they made or sold machine guns, fully automatic handguns, or sawed-off rifles and shotguns.

Then the Federal Firearms Act of 1938 came into being. It attempted to regulate gun manufacture along two fronts. First, it called for all manufacturers of and dealers in arms and ammunition to be licensed with the government. Second, it established regulations governing the shipment of firearms and ammunition between the states and from foreign countries.

The act also made it a crime to transport a stolen gun or a gun whose manufacturer's markings had been removed, obliterated, or altered. Finally, it said that no one could send a gun to a person who had been indicted or

(25)

convicted for a crime punishable by more than a year in prison. The same applied to fugitives from justice.

In the next twenty years, two more regulatory measures were enacted at the federal level. The President, in 1954, was authorized to control the export and import of arms, ammunition, and implements of war, and the Federal Aviation Act of 1958 included a provision that prohibited anyone from bringing a firearm — either concealed or openly — aboard a passenger aircraft.

THE 1960s

All these federal regulations were not aimed at the ordinary American who bought a firearm and took it home. Rather, by attempting to regulate manufacture and distribution, they sought to control the gun before it ever reached the public — or, more precisely, the criminal segments of the public. This approach was in keeping with the long-standing tradition of a law-abiding citizen's need and right to own a firearm.

But then came the 1960s. Everywhere in the land, there seemed to be violence. It poured out of our television and movie screens. It erupted in the streets and on college campuses as thousands of young people voiced their anger over America's involvement in the Vietnam War. It found its way daily into the newspapers in stories of racial disturbances, muggings, robberies, gang rumbles, lovers' quarrels, and family fights. And it exploded in Dallas, Texas, on November 22, 1963, when President John F. Kennedy was killed by a sniper's bullet.

Mr. Kennedy's death shocked the entire nation. But Dallas only marked the beginning of an era of death. On April 4, 1968, a gunman killed civil rights leader Martin Luther King in Memphis, Tennessee. Just two months later — on June 5 — Senator Robert F. Kennedy fell to an assassin's bullet in Los Angeles after winning the California presidential primary election. Critically wounded, the Senator lingered through the night and died the following day.

The violence in the nation and President Kennedy's death triggered a demand in the nation's capital for stronger gun-control legislation. The demand reached its peak in 1968 following the murders of the Reverend Dr. King and Senator Kennedy and during the time of the campus demonstrations against the Vietnam War. The result: federal measures that, slightly more than in the past, had an effect on the law-abiding gun owner.

These federal measures are so important and have become so intertwined with the current gun-control debate that they must have a chapter of their own.

Chapter Four
1968

The major federal legislation that came into being is known as the Gun Control Act of 1968. It takes the place of the old Federal Firearms Act passed in 1938 and consists of two main parts. The two parts are called "Titles."

TWO TITLES

Both Titles contain measures from earlier legislation. As did the National Firearms Act of 1934, Title I attempts to put an end to the underground circulation of guns.

It does so by setting up regulations governing the manufacture, import, and sale of firearms. It calls for all manufacturers, importers, dealers, and pawnbrokers to be licensed by the government. Even a collector of antique firearms (weapons made before 1898) must be licensed. All must pay annual license fees and stick to certain rules when buying and selling. The person who tries to sneak by in the gun business without a license is in for severe penalties.

While Title I hits at underground sales, Title II is aimed at discouraging the manufacture, import, and sale of the weapons most favored by the criminal, chief among them machine guns, sawed-off shotguns, and cheaply made handguns. Taking its lead from the 1938 Act, Title II strikes at such weapons by imposing heavy taxes on their manufacturers and by demanding that their owners register them with the federal government. Harsh penalties can be imposed for failing to register. Title II is also known as The Firearms Act, and in a moment we'll see all the weapons that it covers.

A CAREFUL CONGRESS

When writing the Gun Control Act, the Congress was careful to say that no attempt was being made to keep a law-abiding citizen from owning a gun for a legitimate reason — for sport or self-protection. Rather, Congress stressed that the whole aim was to make it hard for the wrong person to get his or her hands on a gun.

The act became law on December 16, 1968. The Bureau of Alcohol, Tobacco and Firearms (BATF), a branch of the U.S. Treasury Department, was assigned to enforce it. Here now are the act's main provisions as they apply to the buying and selling of firearms.

WHO CAN OWN A GUN?

If you're a law-abiding citizen with a sound mind, there's nothing in the act that prevents you from buying a handgun or a rifle or shotgun for the legal purposes of sport or self-protection.

You must, however, be of a certain age before you can go into a gunshop and make your purchase. The act allows the dealer to sell you a handgun only if you are twenty-one years or older. He can sell you a long gun once you reach eighteen.

But what if you're under eighteen and want to have a long gun for when you go hunting with friends or your dad? You can buy the gun if you have the written permission of a parent or guardian. The only thing the act doesn't want you to do is to get your hands on a gun without your parents knowing.

No matter what your age, you'll need to show the gunshop proof of your identity, your birthdate, and your place of residence. This can usually be done with a driver's license. You'll then be asked to fill out what is called the "Firearms Transaction Record." As its name suggests, it's a form that requires a complete written account of the sale — from your name and address to the make of the gun and its serial number.

WHO MAY NOT OWN A GUN

Title I states that several types of people may not buy, own, or sell a gun.

Heading the list is anyone who is under indictment or has been convicted for a crime that is punishable by more than a year in prison. Next comes anyone who is a fugitive from justice. Then anyone who uses or is addicted to marijuana or narcotics. And then anyone who has been judged mentally defective or has been hospitalized in a mental institution.

It's time now to mention another gun-control measure that Congress passed in 1968 — The Omnibus Crime Control and Safe Streets Act. This act also sought to regulate the manufacture and sale of dangerous firearms, and it listed several types of people who could not legally own guns. Included on the list was any person (1) who had been discharged from military service under dishonorable conditions, (2) who had renounced his or her citizenship, or (3) who was an alien living illegally or unlawfully in the United States.

The Omnibus Act, which was passed early in the year, was later replaced by Title I. The people mentioned in the Omnibus Act were transferred to the Title I list.

WHAT KIND OF GUN
MAY YOU OWN?

You may own any kind of handgun, rifle, or shotgun that is obviously manufactured for legal purposes.

However, guns and what are called "destructive devices" (bombs and the like) are controlled by Title II. These are the weapons that, used so often in crime, are considered the most dangerous of all. They all must be registered with the federal government. You may not buy or own one if it is not registered.

These guns and devices are known as NFA (National Firearms Act) weapons. Making up the list of NFA weapons are:

1. Any weapon that can be concealed on your person. This first rule bears careful reading. It is aimed primarily at just a few types of guns and does *not* apply to conventional, well-made pistols and revolvers. What it does strike at are cheaply made handguns — usually called "Saturday Night Specials" — that seem to be much used in crime, plus gadget-type guns and "pen" guns that look as if they're meant to expel gas but fire a bullet instead.

Foreign manufacturers of cheap handguns have always found the United States to be an excellent customer. One of the major aims of the act was to cut down on the flow of these guns from abroad. We'll be talking more about the Saturday Night Special later.

2. Machine guns.

3. Shotguns manufactured with barrels less than eighteen inches long.

4. Rifles manufactured with barrels less than sixteen inches long. Included here are most pistols with a shoulder stock.

5. Any weapon that comes of cutting a shotgun down to an overall length of twenty-six inches or a barrel length of eighteen inches; any rifle cut down to an overall

(32)

length of twenty-six inches or a barrel length of sixteen inches.

6. Mufflers or silencers for any type of firearm.

7. Destructive devices. This term is used to cover a wide variety of explosives and propellants, including bombs, rockets, cannons, Molotov cocktails, and bazookas.

The purchase of NFA weapons is not actually forbidden, but the regulations set up by the Gun Control Act make it almost impossible for an ordinary person to buy them here or from abroad.

Should you wish to buy an NFA weapon or device, you'll have to make application to the director of the BATF. You'll be called on to submit a photograph of yourself, copies of your fingerprints, and a statement giving the reasons why it is proper or necessary for you to have the weapon (for instance, you may have a collection of World War II firearms who wants to add a bazooka to it.)

Further, along with your own statement, you'll need one from your local police department. In it, the chief of police will have to state that you'll use the weapon for legal purposes only and that your ownership will not be in violation of any of your state and local laws.

As mentioned earlier, all NFA weapons must be registered. If you make, buy, sell, or carry an unregistered one around, you're in for trouble — trouble in the form of a $10,000 fine or up to ten years in prison, or both. Additionally, if you're caught transporting an unregistered NFA weapon, the authorities can confiscate both the weapon and your car. *84- 14874*

Suppose that, unknown to you, there's an NFA weapon tucked away in your attic. What should you do when you come across it? The act calls for you to turn it over to the BATF or your local police department. You will not be allowed to register the weapon. There was a time when you could have done so, but that time came to an end on December 2, 1968.

(33)

WHO CAN SELL YOU A GUN?

With one exception, you may purchase a gun only from someone who is licensed to sell it. The exception? Let's say that you want to buy a gun from a friend who lives down the street. The act isn't against this sort of sale if you're old enough to buy, if you and your friend are not on the list of people forbidden to own guns, and if the purchase won't violate any of your state and local laws. A single sale does not put your friend in the gun business so there's no need for him to be licensed.

But your friend may not sell you the gun if he lives in another state. The act states that, when a gun is sold or shipped to someone over the state line, it must go only to a licensed dealer.

WHERE MAY YOU BUY A GUN?

In general, you may buy a gun only in your own state. You may, however, buy a rifle or a shotgun from a licensed dealer in a state next to yours if your state law permits you to do so and if your purchase is in line with the legal conditions of sale in both states. You may buy ammunition in any state and carry it home with you.

The act also permits you to order a firearm from a licensed out-of-state dealer or manufacturer. But you must arrange to have it sent to a licensed dealer in your state who will then turn it over to you.

Once you own a gun, you may carry it across state lines if you're heading somewhere for sporting purposes. The same applies if you're moving to another state. If you're settling in a new state and own a registered NFA weapon, you must obtain the permission of the BATF before you can move the weapon. If you're moving within your own state, you should notify the Bureau of your new address.

ANOTHER 1968 ACT

Passed in 1968 along with the Gun Control Act was a measure responding to the violent street and campus outbreaks against the Vietnam War. Formally titled The Firearms in Civil Disorders Act — but more popularly known as The Civil Disobedience Act — it contained two main points.

First, the act made it illegal to teach or demonstrate the handling of firearms and explosives to be used in civil disorders. Second, it declared as illegal the acts of transporting or manufacturing for transport any firearm or explosive for use in civil disorders.

To many Americans, the legislation of 1968 seemed strong enough. It seemed to control the use of weapons without interfering too much with the law-abiding citizen who wanted to own a gun for legitimate reasons. Nothing more was required.

But to others, more — much more — was needed if Americans were to be truly safe.

Chapter Five
TWO CAMPS

The wave of violence that washed over the 1960s rolled right into the 1970s. The nation's crime rate continued to rise sharply. Racial strife remained a source of fear. There were further attacks on political leaders. Alabama's Governor George Wallace, while campaigning for the presidency in 1972, was crippled for life by a would-be-assassin's bullet. Two attempts were made to kill President Gerald R. Ford at mid-decade. More and more people bought guns to protect themselves.

The talk of gun control first began in the 1920s "gangster era" during Prohibition and grew in the 1960s. Now, thanks to the violence of the seventies, the topic has captured more public attention than ever before. It is an issue hotly debated from one end of the country to the other, dividing the United States into two sharply opposed camps as people everywhere take sides.

FOR GUN CONTROL

In the first camp are all the people who believe that the Gun Control Act of 1968 just isn't strong enough to do any

(37)

good. They point to the fact that, despite its many regulations, it hasn't reduced by one iota all the crime and violence in the nation.

Nor, they add, are most of today's state and local laws of any real value, being too varied to produce an effective control all across the country. What's the good, they ask, of one city outlawing the gun when all someone need do to buy one is go to another city?

Further, they argue that state and local governments too often don't have the money or the manpower for adequate enforcement. And many local areas don't enforce their laws for fear of angering influential gun owners.

And so a strong federal control is wanted — one that will be equally effective everywhere. Since most people in this camp have nothing against sporting rifles and shotguns, the control is to be directed mainly at handguns. But what form should it take?

There is some disagreement on just what the best control measures would be. Ideally, they should be measures that will do the job and, at the same time, satisfy a public long accustomed to using and liking the gun. There are a number of possibilities.

Some pro-control supporters believe that all handguns — and not just those on the NFA list — should be registered with the federal government. Registration will make the job of tracing the owner of a gun used in a crime easier. Some opinion favors extending the registration to rifles and shotguns.

Other pro-control people think that all handgun owners should be made to obtain licenses. Like registration, licensing will help trace the owners of guns involved in crimes. It will also make it harder for someone forbidden ownership by present law to buy a gun.

Still others think that the ownership of handguns should be banned — but only in areas known to have exceptionally high crime rates.

And still others look forward to the day when handguns will be outlawed everywhere in the nation and their owners made to surrender or sell them to the government.

This camp also wants to see state and local laws strengthened and enforced. Effective laws at these levels are needed for two reasons. First, they can be passed more quickly than a law meant to embrace the entire nation and can be used to good advantage until some truly strong federal legislation comes along. Second, the best control will come from a combination of federal, state, and local laws, all supporting each other.

AGAINST GUN CONTROL

The anti-gun-control camp is manned by people who hold two basic beliefs.

First, they contend that the Constitution guarantees every law-abiding American the right to own a gun; laws banning firearms will violate that right. Second, they argue that controls will not work — that the registration, licensing, or banning of guns will do nothing to reduce the crime and violence so rampant in the United States.

They point to the Second Amendment — "the right of the people to keep and bear arms shall not be infringed" — to substantiate their belief in a constitutional guarantee. Then they explain their second belief this way:

Criminals will neither register their guns nor obtain licenses. Thus, the laws will be of no help in finding the weapons and people that cause all the trouble. Nor will criminals turn in their guns if firearms are banned. Only law-abiding citizens will do so, and they'll be left more vulnerable than ever before to criminal attack. They'll also be defenseless against foreign invasion and dictatorial suppression at home.

The anti-control camp holds that criminals and not guns cause all the trouble. The gun is simply a tool and is

(39)

not lethal until it is held in someone's hand. And so the best way to reduce crime and violence is not to act against the gun. Rather, make the criminal the target. Enforce the present laws against him. Enact even stronger ones.

And what of the many people who accidentally wound or kill themselves or others? Again, the anti-control camp believes that the gun itself is not at fault, is not dangerous until picked up. The tragic problem can best be solved by local or nationwide programs that instruct the public in the safe use of firearms.

THE LEADERS

As will happen in any national debate, certain individuals and organizations have emerged as the leaders of the two camps.

Among the national political figures who immediately took the lead for stricter gun controls were Massachusetts Senator Edward Kennedy, who had lost two brothers to assassins; Senator Birch Bayh of Indiana; Senator Hiram Fong of Hawaii; Representative Jonathan B. Bingham of New York; and Representative Abner K. Mikva of Illinois. They all pressed for legislation that we'll be looking at in detail later. The legislation reflected the differing views among the pro-control people on how best to handle the problem. It ranged from measures calling for the registration of all handguns to those banning handguns to the general public.

One representative — Ron Dellums of California — went so far as to author a bill that would ban from sale all toys that were copies of or resembled firearms and destructive devices.

On the opposite side of the fence were such figures as Senator Barry Goldwater of Arizona, Senator James A. McClure of Idaho, and Representative Steve Symms, also of Idaho. They argued vehemently against the various control measures being proposed. Senator Goldwater warned taxpayers that any national program of gun registration would cost several billion dollars just to start. In early 1977, Representative Symms presented a bill calling for the repeal of the Gun Control Act of 1968.

As the debate grew more heated, a number of organizations took shape at the local and national levels. Citizen groups in support of stricter controls sprang up throughout the nation, especially in California, Illinois, Ohio, Michigan, Massachusetts, and Rhode Island. Among them were the Committee for Handgun Control in Illinois, People Versus Handguns in Massachusetts, and Citizens to Save Lives in Michigan. A principal aim of these many groups was to educate the public on the dangers of the gun and to stress the need for control.

But some took an active hand in pushing for legislation. The Committee for Handgun Control, for instance, sought to have the U.S. Consumer Product Safety Committee hold hearings in 1975 on whether handgun ammunition should be banned from public sale as a "hazardous substance." The Committee for Handgun Control hoped that once the ammunition disappeared, the handgun would soon follow suit. Due in great part to the opposition led by Representative Steve Symms, the committee's effort to win the ban failed.

Both the Citizens to Save Lives and the People Versus Handguns committees involved themselves in state elections. Both worked diligently to place strong control measures before the voters in Michigan and Massachusetts.

Two organizations appeared at the national level. The first was the National Coalition to Ban Handguns, which was formed by several small gun-control groups to gain greater strength. As did the state groups, it served as an educational outlet. Headquartered today in Washington, D.C., the coalition conducts a nationwide information program on the need to rid the United States of all handguns.

(41)

The second organization — The National Council to Control Handguns (NCCH) — moved in a different direction. Established in 1974, it registered itself as a lobby organization in the nation's capital. As a lobby, it has pressed Congress, the states, and the cities for the passage of tough handgun controls.

The NCCH was founded by marketing executive Nelson T. Shields III and several friends after Shields's son was fatally shot by an unknown assailant while standing on a San Francisco street. The elder Shields, wanting to help others avoid the tragedy that had befallen his family, began to study gun control and was appalled to find that no one was lobbying in Congress on its behalf. The result: the formation of the NCCH.

With the National Coalition to Ban Handguns, the NCCH is aiming for the eventual banning of all handguns in the United States.

The leading organization fighting gun control is the National Rifle Association (NRA). Founded in 1871 by a group of National Guard officers who were concerned over the poor marksmanship seen in the military of that day, it is the oldest sportsmen's organization in the United States. Its membership numbers more than a million sports shooters, hunters, gun dealers, gun makers, and collectors.

The NRA promotes good marksmanship, governs competitive sports shooting throughout the country, and sponsors hunter-training programs. It believes in the right of gun ownership for lawful purposes and, from its headquarters in Washington, D.C., has long worked in three ways against gun control.

First, it operates as a lobby in Congress and at the state and local levels. In its own words, its aim here is to defeat any legislation that "would deprive citizens of their rights to purchase, own, or use firearms for legitimate sporting and defensive purposes."

Second, the NRA reports on all gun-control legislation — from the local to the national level — in its official publication, *The American Rifleman*. The magazine urges every NRA member to write his legislators and advise a vote against all such legislation. The write-in tactic is seen as a powerful political weapon, with up to one million members saying in effect to their government representatives, "Your vote for gun control means our vote against you in the next election."

Finally, the organization administers what is known as the NRA Political Victory Fund. The NRA describes the fund as "a political action committee." The fund assists in the election of political candidates against gun control and, again in the NRA's words, works "to defeat politicians who disregard the rights of law-abiding firearms owners."

These, then, are the major contestants in the debate. In a later chapter, we'll be seeing more of what they're doing and saying. But now, because we've just scratched the surface of their beliefs, let's take a closer look at exactly why they're for or against gun control.

Chapter Six
A BASIC QUESTION

Just as there are two sides in the debate, so are there two main areas of discussion. The first area centers on the arguments for and against the idea of gun control itself. In the second are the arguments for and against the laws being proposed to control guns.

In this chapter and the next, we'll be looking at the main arguments for and against control itself. To start, we have to go back to the U.S. Constitution.

THE GUN AND THE CONSTITUTION

> A well-regulated militia being
> necessary to the security of
> a free State, the right of the
> people to keep and bear arms
> shall not be infringed.

Making up the Second Amendment to the Constitution, these twenty-seven words have triggered one of the most basic questions — if not *the* most basic one — in the debate. Does the country have the right to control the

(45)

ownership and use of guns, or will controls deprive Americans of a constitutional right?

The answer depends on how you interpret the meaning of the Second Amendment. Anti-control supporters believe that it gives every American the right to have and keep a gun of his own. The pro-control group says that the amendment, by mentioning "a well-regulated militia," limits the bearing of arms to members of the state militias, now called the National Guard. Further, it limits the use of arms to the defense of the country.

Here now are the "whys" behind these conflicting beliefs.

THE ANTI-CONTROL ARGUMENT

When writing the Constitution, the Founding Fathers authorized the federal government to maintain a standing army. But, remembering so well how the British king had used his troops to suppress the Colonies before the Revolution, they were suspicious of any standing army, even one of their own making. If it fell into the hands of some future despot, he could use it as a mighty tool against the people.

And so the Founding Fathers agreed that the federal force was to be a small one. The country's main line of defense against foreign invasion or the suppressions of a despot would be its various state militias, all of them made up of civilians who could quickly become soldiers in times of danger.

The Second Amendment paved the way for citizens to carry their own guns in these militias. But the amendment was not meant to say that the militia members were the *only* citizens to have guns. This point is clearly indicated in the writings of Alexander Hamilton.

Hamilton wrote that, actually, there were to be two militias. One was to be "organized" — namely, manned

(46)

by the citizen soldiers. The other was to be "unorganized" and made up of the rest of the population.

Hamilton's views can leave little doubt that the Second Amendment was intended to give *all* Americans the right to own a gun. And there can be no doubt left whatsoever when we learn of a later action taken by Congress. Shortly after the amendment was adopted, a proposal was made to add four words to it. They would have altered it to read: ". . . the right of the people to bear arms *for the common defense* shall not be infringed."

Congress soundly defeated the proposal. The right of ownership was not to be just for the "common defense," or, as we would say today, national defense. A man had the right to own a gun for any legitimate purpose.

It also must be remembered that American law is much based on English Common Law and on the English Bill of Rights of 1689. Both give a man the right to keep arms for the defense of his country and himself.

And it's especially important to remember the name of William Blackstone. A distinguished lawyer of the eighteenth century, he brilliantly explained English law in a series of books called the *Commentaries*. In them, he said that the ownership of weapons for national and personal defense was "an absolute right of individuals." The Founding Fathers admired Blackstone and referred often to his works when drafting the Constitution and its amendments.

In the light of all these facts, it is clear that every American has the constitutionally guaranteed right to own a gun for any legitimate reason — for defense against foreign invasion, for defense against a suppressive government at home, and for the protection of himself, his family, and his home against criminal attack. Any control measure that interferes with that right is against the laws of the United States.

One point should be remembered about defending yourself against a suppressive government at home. Even though the National Guards are state armies, their commander-in-chief is the President, and he may order them "federalized" at any time. In the hands of the wrong president, they could be taken and turned against the very people whom they were initially designed to protect. Further, the federal government retains full ownership and control of all National Guard arms.

THE PRO-CONTROL ARGUMENT

On five occasions, the U.S. Supreme Court has considered cases involving a citizen's "right" to own guns. On all five occasions, it has interpreted the Second Amendment as applying only to the bearing of arms by a militia. In the Court's opinion, the right of an individual to own a firearm for his own purposes is not guaranteed in the Constitution. Steps to control gun ownership and use are perfectly legal.

Further, as the American Bar Association points out, every federal court, when faced with similar cases, has come to the same conclusion. The courts have also held that the firearms laws already enacted under the police laws of the states are constitutional.

In all, when a citizen owns a gun, he is not exercising a constitutionally guaranteed right. He is exercising a privilege. When the privilege becomes dangerous to the common good, there is nothing to prevent the state and federal governments from restricting it or taking it away altogether.

It may have been necessary at one point in our history to keep the ordinary citizen armed for the country's defense. But times have changed. That sort of defense is no longer necessary or effective. Nelson Shields of the National Council to Control Handguns comments on this point by saying that our Army, Navy, Air Force, and National Guard will defend us if we're attacked from the outside. He says that they're the ones best equipped for the job — not a mass of citizens with guns.

It must be remembered, too, that gun control is aimed primarily at the handgun. Shields says that a citizenry armed with handguns wouldn't be very effective against an invading force. Handguns, he says, aren't much good against targets beyond fifty feet away — especially if those targets are trained soldiers with machine guns and rifles.

And what if the federal government should move to suppress the people? What if a dictator should take over? We have many safeguards against such threats — the ballot, our democratic traditions, an alert and outspoken press, and the federal government's system of "checks and balances." We are wiser to place our trust in these safeguards and to work for their preservation than to depend on the privately owned gun.

Finally — even if gun ownership were a right — it could never reasonably be considered an absolute right. If it were, then any American could own such weapons as machine guns, bazookas, and howitzers, and no one could do a thing about it. The situation would not only be intolerably dangerous but ridiculous. The government has the duty — and the right — to protect the people against such a possibility.

Chapter Seuen

THREE MORE ARGUMENTS

Thus far, the talk has been mostly about defending ourselves against invasion from without and suppression from within. But what of keeping firearms for self-protection against criminal attack?

This question brings us to the first of the next major arguments. They all concern the handgun.

THE GUN AND SELF-PROTECTION

Anti-control supporters believe that the law-abiding citizen needs the handgun to protect himself and his family. No ordinary man should be expected to take on an armed assailant bare-handed; that's fine for television heroes, but he's a peaceful citizen not trained in hand-to-hand fighting and he's much too apt to be killed or injured for life. And a woman, of course, is especially vulnerable to attack unless she has some means of defending herself.

One of the main anti-control arguments is that, when criminals know that someone can handle a gun, they are far less willing to make him or her their victim.

Pro-control supporters counter by saying that the citizen who owns a gun for self-protection is far more likely to wound or kill a loved one or a friend than a criminal.

The Anti-Control Argument

The knowledge that a person knows how to defend himself with a gun is in itself a deterrent to crime. This has been proved in the city of Orlando, Florida, where the crime rate quickly fell after the police held a series of classes that trained 6000 women in self-defense with firearms.

The classes ran from September 1966 to May 1967. In the first three months of 1967, there were only three forcible rapes in the city as compared to thirty-three for the same months in 1966. The overall crime rate dropped from 17.1 to 8.1 per 100,000 population. Orlando was the only major American city to show a decrease in crime during 1967.

Highland Park, Michigan, reports a similar experience. In 1967, the police conducted a well-publicized program of firearms training for the city's merchants. There wasn't a single store robbery attempted in town during the following four months.

As everyone should agree, it's far better to keep someone from attacking you in the first place than to stop him once he's started. It's impossible, of course, to prove that an attacker does not strike because he knows that you have — or might have — a way to defend yourself. But studies have shown that robbery rates are always highest in those areas where people are least likely to be armed.

New York City, for instance, has control laws so strict that it's almost impossible for the average citizen to own a gun legally. Very few law-abiding citizens there are armed. But the city has the highest robbery rate in the country. Twenty percent of all robberies in the U.S. occur in New York.

(*Author's note:* Pro-control advocates counter this argument by saying that New York City has the second lowest murder rate of the nation's ten largest cities and that its crime rate is falling yearly. They then point to a BATF study that shows that 96 percent of the guns traced in New York crime have been brought in from outside the city. Hence, the need for uniform control all across the country.)

It is true that innocent people are often shot accidentally. And that many are shot by mistake by frightened householders who think them to be burglars. But this problem can be solved not by taking the gun away but by educational programs that train the public in its safe use.

The Pro-Control Argument

You need only look to a 1973 study to see that the gun is too dangerous a weapon to be kept around the house for self-protection. The study, made by two Ohio coroners and two professors from Case Western Reserve University, shows that:

A gun kept for protection is six times more likely to kill someone you know rather than an attacker. Seventy percent of the people killed by handguns are shot by relatives or acquaintances.

The same warning has come from the National Commission on the Causes and Prevention of Violence, which was formed in 1968 by President Lyndon B. Johnson. The commission reported that, for every burglar stopped by a gun, four gun owners or members of their families are killed in firearms accidents.

The National Council for the Control of Handguns points to yet another danger. For the most part, the gun is actually useless as a defense against burglars because 90 percent of all housebreaks are committed when the

RANK	in the 50 largest cities	CITY	PROBABILITY

HOMICIDE RISK IN SELECTED MAJOR CITIES
(Per MIT study for National Science Foundation)

RANK	in the 50 largest cities	CITY	PROBABILITY
1		Atlanta	1 in 25
2		Detroit	1 in 32
4		Newark, N.J.	1 in 33
6		Washington, D.C.	1 in 36
7		St. Louis	1 in 36
8		Miami	1 in 46
11		Dallas	1 in 50
14		Oakland	1 in 53
19		New York City	1 in 60
20		Memphis	1 in 70
23		Denver	1 in 73
41		Seattle	1 in 151

tenants are away. The gun is among the items usually stolen. It then makes its way into the underworld and contributes to the increase of crime and violence in the nation. The BATF reports that an estimated 100,000 hand-guns are stolen each year.

In all, it's nonsense to say that the gun protects. Rather, it injures or kills innocent people in accidental and mistaken shootings. And it is too likely to be stolen and passed into the underworld.

THE GUN AND CRIME

Anti-control supporters contend that tough laws against the gun will not reduce crime and violence in the United States. They put their argument in the simplest of terms: The gun by itself doesn't kill or commit some other crime. People do. So act against the gunman, not the gun.

The pro-control camp agrees that, by itself, the gun doesn't kill. But they point out that people *with* guns do the most robbing and killing in the United States.

The Anti-Control Argument

The opposition makes it sound as if practically every American who owns a handgun is about to commit a crime or kill someone with it. This just isn't true. The vast majority of American gun owners are sensible, law-abiding citizens and not trigger-happy fools. They're not responsible for most of the crime and violence in our country. Just listen to what President Gerald R. Ford said in the mid-1970s:

"A small percentage of the entire population accounts for a very large proportion of the vicious crimes committed. Most serious crimes are committed by repeaters. These relatively few persistent criminals who cause so much worry and fear are the core of the problem. . . .

"To illustrate the nature of this problem, let me point out that, in one city, over sixty rapes, more than 200 burglaries, and fourteen murders were committed by only ten persons in less than twelve months. Unfortunately, this example is not unique."

Mr. Ford's point is substantiated by a Chicago study made in 1974. The study, which analyzed 970 murders there, showed that over 60 percent of the killers had prior criminal records. More than half of their victims had records.

Further proof comes from Michigan. The head of the Michigan State Police says that less than 1/100th of 1 percent of the guns used in crime there are owned by law-abiding citizens.

Statistics such as these can leave no doubt that most crime in the country is committed by just a few people. To take guns away from the law-abiding citizen will not cut down on the crime, the violence, and the killing. It will only render him defenseless against the country's small — but ever growing — criminal class. The criminals certainly won't give up their guns.

(55)

There is another fact that must be faced. The American court system has been too lenient with criminals in recent years. It has been too eager to give them "a break" when they are tried for their first offenses, often doling out minimal sentences or choosing probation rather than imprisonment. Instead of punishing the troublemakers and separating them from society, it has tried too hard to "rehabilitate" them. It has too often allowed the guilty to go free on some technicality in the law.

This attitude has been much responsible for the growth of crime in the United States. The would-be criminal quickly realizes that he's going to be pretty safe from severe punishment. So why shouldn't he make trouble?

Senator Barry Goldwater, writing in a 1975 issue of the *Reader's Digest* magazine, comments on the situation. He reports that in Washington, D.C., 184 persons were convicted for gun possession during a six-month period that year. Only 14 were sentenced.

The Senator adds that, in another city with strict gun controls, only one out of six people convicted of crimes involving a gun were sent to prison.

Senator Goldwater believes that it is time for the American public to crack down on both the court system and the criminal. Judges should be told that the public expects them to deal sternly with criminals or be removed from the bench. Stiffer laws against criminal activity should be adopted and enforced.

In all, a crackdown on the criminal and not the gun is the real answer to the problem.

The Pro-Control Argument

We agree that the handgun is harmless until someone picks it up. But, once held in the human hand, it becomes the weapon *most often* used in crime and the weapon *most responsible* for murders in this country.

(56)

Remember the statistics that were given in chapter one — that 51 percent of all our murders are committed with the handgun. Each year it is also involved in 150,000 armed robberies, 10,000 suicides, and 2,700 accidental deaths.

Most handgun murders in the United States are not committed by criminals. Rather, as the FBI reported in 1975, almost 70 percent of the country's murders were committed by family members or acquaintances. FBI statistics in 1980 showed these figures to be down to 51 percent. These murders are known as "crimes of passion" because they occur when someone so loses his temper during a flare-up that he grabs a gun in a blind rage.

Why is the handgun such a popular murder weapon? Basically because, from the killer's standpoint, it is a "safe" weapon. It can be fired at a distance. The assailant need not have bodily contact with his victim and run the risk

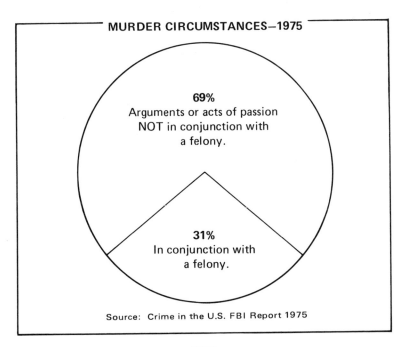

MURDER CIRCUMSTANCES—1975

69%
Arguments or acts of passion
NOT in conjunction with
a felony.

31%
In conjunction with
a felony.

Source: Crime in the U.S. FBI Report 1975

of injury to himself, as would be the case if he picked up a baseball bat or tried to settle things with his fists. And it's deadly; the person who is shot isn't likely to get up off the floor and attack the gunman. *Conclusion*

There's only one way to stop the senseless "crimes of passion" — and that's to remove the handgun from reach. Then it won't be readily at hand when someone flies into a rage. He'll have to think twice before attacking. He'll have to find another weapon. All this will give him the time to cool down. A life will be saved.

These same facts work for suicide. A person about to take his life might have the time to reconsider if he can't simply walk to a bureau drawer and take out a gun. And nothing needs to be said about the accidents that will be prevented once the handgun is out of reach.

Now let's turn from the ordinary citizen to the actual criminal. The causes of crime and violence in our society are many and complex. To cite just two, there is, first, the rapid growth of our cities, which is throwing millions of people together in crowded and uncomfortable circumstances. And there is the sad fact that so many of our people have so much money and so many advantages while just as many of our people are forced to live in poverty, held there by such factors as racial discrimination and poor educational opportunities.

If crime and violence are to be reduced, these problems and many others must be solved. Strong and firmly enforced laws against the criminal, as helpful as they can be, won't do the whole job. But it's going to take years to solve these problems — perhaps even several generations. Controls against the handgun, however, can be swiftly enacted and can do much to cut down on crime and violence in the meantime. The controls can then go right on doing an effective job after the problems have been partially or totally solved.

(58)

It must also be remembered that strong laws against the criminal will do nothing to prevent "crimes of passion." There is no law that can keep a man from flying into a rage. Only strong controls, putting the handgun out of his reach, can take care of things.

BUT DO GUN LAWS REALLY WORK?

This is one of the most hotly argued questions in the whole debate.

Pro-control supporters do not believe the opposition's argument that future controls won't work because the criminal won't obey them. They contend that, whenever U.S. cities have enacted tough control laws and then enforced them, the murder rates there have dropped. Further, all foreign nations with strict controls have lower crime rates than we; it's time that we learned a lesson from them.

The anti-control camp answers that, in many cities with strong gun laws, the murder rates have actually gone up. So far as other countries are concerned, the controls have little to do with the low crime rates there. Crime rates in other nations depend more on the nature of the people and their traditions than on control laws.

The Pro-Control Argument

The recent experiences of two large American cities have proved how effective controls can be. The cities are Philadelphia, Pennsylvania, and Toledo, Ohio.

Alarmed at its crime rate, Philadelphia in 1965, passed a law requiring every citizen to furnish the police department with fingerprints and a photograph when obtaining a permit to buy a gun. In one year alone, the law exposed twenty-seven applicants who had once been convicted on "intent-to-kill" charges; sixty-nine with past rec-

(59)

ords for carrying concealed weapons; and close to 200 with robbery, theft, rape, and narcotics addiction records. While firearms are now responsible for 66 percent of the murders committed in America, they are responsible only 58 percent of the time in Philadelphia.

In 1968, Toledo passed a similar law. Two years later, the handgun murder rate in the city that was once known as "the gun capital of the midwest" had dropped twenty-two percentage points. Need more be said?

Now for foreign countries: Starting with Great Britain, the homicide rates speak for themselves.

The rate in England and Wales in the early 1970s, for instance, stood at an astonishingly low 0.04 people per 100,000 population; the rate for Scotland was 0.1. In 1971, with a population of about 50 million, England and Wales had only 35 homicides with firearms, while the United States, with 207 million people, had 12,243 such killings — or about eighty-five times as many. London reported only 2 handgun murders in 1972.

Great Britain requires that every citizen receive a certificate of competence before buying or owning a gun. The British feel that their low homicide rates are due to the fact that the authorities have been successful in keeping people from carrying "offensive weapons" and have punished those who don't obey the laws.

The murder rate in Japan is even lower than in Great Britain. It stood at 0.02 per 100,000 population in the late 1960s. During 1972, this island country of 107 million people had only 28 handgun murders; the United States suffered 10,017 handgun slayings that year. The city of Tokyo reported only 3 handgun murders in 1970 and only one in 1971.

Japan completely outlaws the possession of handguns by private citizens.

Great Britain and Japan are not just isolated examples. The following chart clearly shows the effectiveness of gun-control laws by comparing the homicide rates in twelve foreign countries with those in the United States. The rates are based on 100,000 population.

What kinds of control laws do these countries have? They all require gun owners to be licensed and/or call for the registration of all firearms. In France, anyone who plans to buy a gun must first undergo an intensive police investigation. The Netherlands requires a permit for all firearms. In Australia, all shotguns and .22 rifles must be registered; pistols and rifles must be registered and their owners must have licenses.

In addition, there are five European countries that, like Japan, totally prohibit the private ownership of handguns. They are Albania, Cyprus, Greece, Ireland, and the Soviet Union.

Gun-control laws have all worked to reduce crime in these countries. They can do the same for us.

The Anti-Control Argument

Two facts prove that controls don't work. First, a chief aim of the 1968 Gun Control Act was to cut the flow of cheap handguns from abroad; the imports did fall off somewhat for a time, *but* they very quickly rose back to their previous levels because of importing of weapons not on the prohibited list. Second, the homicide rate in our nation has jumped 300 percent since the passage of the act.

Now let's look at those two cities — Philadelphia and Toledo — where the murder rates are supposed to have dropped. FBI statistics show that *exactly the opposite* happened.

The FBI reports that the murder rate in Philadelphia stood at 5.4 people per 100,000 population in 1964, the year before the city's control law went on the books. By 1973, the rate had jumped to 11.5. The 1964 robbery rate

WORLDWIDE HANDGUN OWNERS*—1968
(Per 100,000 population)

U.S.A.	13,500
Canada	
Austria	3,000
Israel	1,000
Netherlands	under 500
Great Britain	under 500
Ireland	under 500
Finland	under 500
Greece	under 500
Switzerland	Insignificant

*Note apparent correlation with Homicide rates.

Source: 1968 Eisenhower Commission

WORLD HOMICIDE RATES BY FIREARMS
(Per 100,000 population)

U.S.A.—1974	6.6
—1971	5.6
—1968	4.5
Australia—1970	0.6
Canada—1963	0.5
Italy—1968	0.5
New Zealand—1969	0.3
France—1969	0.3
Germany—1970	0.3
Switzerland—1970	0.2
Denmark—1969	0.2
Netherlands—1970	0.1
Scotland—1970	0.1
Eng. & Wales*—1970	0.04
Japan*—1968	0.02

*London had two HANDGUN murders in 1972; in 1971 Tokyo had only one!

Source: 1968 Eisenhower Commission

was 75.2 per 100,000 population. It rose to 232.6 by 1973.

In light of these figures, it means little to say that firearms are used as murder weapons only 58 percent of the time in Philadelphia as compared with 66 percent for the nation as a whole. What counts is that the city's murder and robbery rates have been going up despite the law. It just didn't work.

As for Toledo, the FBI reports that twenty-six handgun murders were committed there during 1968, but that handgun murders numbered thirty-six in 1972, and sixty-two in 1973.

The pro-control supporters just don't tell you the whole story when they say that Toledo's murder rate dropped 22 percent. It's quite possible to have the percentage of murders by handgun go down while, at the same time, have the number of people killed by handguns go up.

For instance, using round figures, if twenty out of forty murders were committed with handguns in one year, that would mean that handguns were used in 50 percent of the murders committed. But thirty handgun murders out of ninety killings in the next year would equal 30 percent — or a drop of twenty percentage points. Our opponents "forgot" to mention all this and omitted the fact that more people than ever before were handgun victims. Again, a control law failed to work.

(*Author's note*: Conflicting statistics such as we've run into here can be maddening when you're trying to get a clear and factual picture of a situation. All that can be said is that neither side is lying, but that statistics can always be found to support almost *any* argument. There seems just one way for someone to handle the problem, and that's to know that there's some truth on either side and then try to judge which statistics contribute to the truest picture.)

(63)

Now what about foreign homicide rates? The fact is, you don't tell the whole story when you simply compare our firearms homicide rates with those of other countries. First, you fail to take into consideration the cultural differences that are involved. Second, you fail to consider the overall murder rates in the other countries.

Culturally, some people seem less prone to commit crimes than others. The Japanese are a prime example. Certainly, there were only three handgun murders in Tokyo during 1970. But you should also know that there was a total of only *213 murders of any kind* in Tokyo that year, giving it an extremely low 1.9 overall murder rate. When you live in a city that has a very low overall murder rate, you're bound to have fewer handgun murders, regardless of whether you have or don't have strict control laws.

Further, the Japanese living here in America seem just as disinclined to commit murder as those living in gun-controlled Tokyo. In fact, the citizens of Tokyo, with their 1.9 rate, commit twice as many murders as Japanese-Americans. FBI figures show that the murder arrest rate in 1972 for Japanese-Americans was 0.9 per 100,000 of their people. In 1973, it was .07.

Any number of cultural factors — ranging from quiet natures to moral scruples and individual codes of conduct — may be at work in any of the gun-controlled countries and may be the very things that are keeping the murder rates low. The rates will remain low not for as long as there are control laws, but only for as long as these cultural factors remain in force.

These very factors are at work among millions of peaceful, law-abiding Americans. Yet we are accused of being a violent nation. The truth of the matter, as said before, is that only a relatively small percentage of our people are responsible for most of the trouble. The vast majority of Americans don't need gun controls to help them behave themselves. What we must do instead is work against the criminal element and, at the same time, try to overcome the many social and economic ills that have triggered today's increased crime and violence.

Chapter Eight

AGAINST MANUFACTURE

As I noted in chapter five, the pro-control camp wants strong handgun measures passed at the federal level. But there are varied opinions on just what would be the best measures. Pro-control supporters, depending on their personal views, are asking for laws that range from a nationwide registration of handguns to an outright banning of these weapons.

If you're a legislator who hopes to control the handgun, there are three approaches open to you. You can work for laws that will restrict manufacture, importation, and sale of handguns. Or you can work for laws that will prohibit the general public from owning the gun. Or, of course, you can try for laws that combine the above two approaches.

In this chapter, we'll look at what can be done to control handgun manufacture, importation, and sale. At the same time, we'll see what some legislators have tried to do along this line.

CONTROLLING MANUFACTURE
AND DISTRIBUTION

Were you a legislator in favor of controlling manufacture and distribution, you'd be out to prevent the handgun — or at least certain of its most dangerous models — from ever reaching the public in the first place. You'd aim to cut down on the supply from U.S. factories and from overseas.

You could try any of several basic types of control:

You could prohibit the production of: (1) all handguns for general public ownership; (2) those handguns most easily concealed on the criminal; or (3) the cheapest of handguns — the so-called Saturday Night Specials. Or, if you did not wish to stop production itself, you could (4) stringently control handgun distribution through a system of licensing all people in the firearms business.

GENERAL PRODUCTION

This is the most extreme type of control. No manufacturer would be able to make a handgun that could be legally sold to a citizen. You would, however, permit manufacturers to go on producing handguns for police, military, and limited sports use.

A prohibition of general handgun manufacture would hit the arms industry hard. Decreased production would cost thousands of factory workers their jobs. Allied workers — from shippers to dealers — would be equally hurt. Manufacturers, suppliers of parts, and gunshops would face an immense loss of profits.

These consequences — plus the anger that's sure to come from gun sportsmen and the countless Americans who believe in a constitutionally guaranteed right to own a firearm — make it difficult for any legislator to think

(68)

about banning general production. You'd be in especially deep trouble if you represented an area that depends a great deal on arms manufacture for a living. Call for a ban and you could count on a heavy vote against you in the next election.

And so, in deciding on this approach, you'd need to answer one overriding question. Will the economic suffering caused by a total ban be worth the reduction in crime and violence that might be brought about?

THE CONCEALED WEAPON

In a recent study, the BATF looked at the kinds of handguns that the police are asked to trace after an armed crime has been committed. The Bureau found that 71 percent had a barrel length of three inches or less. Sixty-one percent had a caliber of .32 or less.

It's no big secret that what the criminal likes best is a handgun that can be hidden in his clothing without making a "suspicious bulge," and that is lightweight enough so that he can whip it out easily. What the study did was find out what size gun was used most often in crime.

Your approach now would be not to prohibit the manufacture of all guns, but only those of approximately this inviting size. Larger models could still be legally made and sold.

In the light of the BATF's findings, it would seem obvious to prohibit handguns with a barrel length of three inches or less. But this won't work. To get around the law, all a criminal would have to do is buy a larger gun and then cut the barrel down to the desired length.

The approach, instead, calls for a gun of a certain *overall* size to be prohibited. Both the barrel and the frame sizes are taken into consideration, with the frame size being the more important of the two. Some gun-control advocates feel that a handgun should have at least a 5¾-

inch frame and a 4-inch barrel before it can be manufactured. In an effort to keep the gun from being sold too cheaply, they also want it to contain safety features and materials of a certain quality.

The approach is intended to discourage the criminal use of the gun in two ways. First, a gun with a larger frame size will be just that much more difficult to carry concealed. Second, if it is well manufactured from quality materials, it may be expensive enough to keep many criminals — especially newcomers — from buying it.

The obvious drawback is that a larger handgun can still be carried concealed, even if with added difficulty. The criminal might be willing to take a chance with a bigger model.

A ban on the small handgun is bound to get you into trouble with manufacturers, particularly if you call for a 5 3/4-inch frame and a 4-inch barrel. More than 70 percent of the handguns being manufactured today are smaller than this size. Factories would have to be retooled before larger handguns could be made. Retooling is an expensive process. Some manufacturers might never be able to afford the job. Some might take years before getting to it.

All this would certainly cut down on the number of guns reaching the public market. But there's a question of fairness that you'd have to answer to your satisfaction. The companies least able to afford retooling would be small manufacturers. Would it be fair to hit them so hard — and perhaps even put them out of business — while giving large companies with the money to retool a clear field in the handgun business?

THE SATURDAY NIGHT SPECIAL

Your target here is just one kind of handgun. It is the cheapest of weapons, short in the barrel, low in caliber,

and made of inferior materials. Because it can be purchased for just a few dollars, it is thought to be a particular
favorite with criminals. It gets its name from the fact that
even a "part-time" thug who is out to cause trouble over
the weekend can afford to buy it.

Should you attempt to ban the manufacture of Saturday Night Specials, you'll run into objections from many
pro-control advocates. They'll tell you that, in going after
this one gun alone, you're really doing nothing to reduce
crime.

Why? Because, though it has a bad reputation, it
doesn't seem to be used in all that many crimes. The New
York City police department has reported that only 30 percent of the handguns that it confiscates are Specials. The
handguns most used in crimes are of good quality, as are
the majority of the 40 million handguns owned in the
United States.

Further, a ban on the Special's manufacture will not
have a long-range effect. Take the Special off the market
and the criminal will simply buy a slightly more expensive
weapon and get on with his "work."

You will get some support, however, from those pro-
control advocates who see the banning of the Special as
one step along the way to the eventual control of all guns.
But then you'll hear others predict that, once such legislation is passed, Congress will not then move on to stricter
laws. Gun control is a controversial issue that makes many
politicians nervous. They could well use a Special law as a
"cosmetic" measure to kid the public into thinking that
they've solved things when, in reality, they've avoided
facing up to the really tough issues of control.

And there's another problem. Before you can move
for legislation, you'll have to come up with a good definition of just what the Saturday Night Special is. There are
presently several definitions given for the gun. But none
really seem to cover all the bases. Some concentrate on

(71)

size. Some on design. And some on materials. You'll need a definition that is both broad and concise. Otherwise, manufacturers may find a loophole that will enable them to turn out guns just as cheap as the one you're banning.

LICENSING

Now suppose that you don't wish to prohibit gun production itself. You're willing to see guns made and sold, but you'd like to control their distribution in a way that would make it difficult for troublemakers to get them.

You might try to see that only responsible manufacturers, importers, and dealers are able to engage in the firearms business. You would — as do our present laws — call for all these people to be licensed. But there the similarity would end. You'd have the licenses cost far more than they do at present.

Today's fees are so low that anybody can afford a license to go into the firearms business. The annual license fee for a gun manufacturer or importer is $50. A dealer pays $10 a year; a gunsmith, $10; and a pawnbroker, $25.

Because their annual fee is just $10, there are more than 150,000 dealers in the United States at present. The BATF estimates that, of all these license holders, only 20,000 to 30,000 are serious, professional dealers. Many of the others buy a license just to make it easy for them to sell or trade guns from time to time. Still others are suspected of dealing with the underworld; they happily spend a few dollars a year to give themselves the appearance of being legitimate businessmen.

With so many people now in the gun business, the enforcement of the existing control laws is always difficult and, at times, impossible. Hopefully, heavy license fees would thin their ranks to just those who are reputable.

LEGISLATION AGAINST THE GUN

The 1970s saw a number of congressional leaders propose laws that would restrict or totally ban the manufacture of handguns.

A Total Ban

In the mid 1970s, at least fifteen bills calling for a total ban on manufacture were introduced in the House of Representatives, and one in the Senate. Typical of them all were bills that were presented by Representative Jonathan B. Bingham of New York, Representative Abner J. Mikva of Illinois, and Delegate Walter E. Fauntroy of the District of Columbia.

Each of these three bills would prohibit the manufacture, importation, and sale not only of all handguns but of their ammunition as well. They would also prohibit the purchase and ownership of handguns and ammunition by the general public. Handgun owners would be asked to turn their weapons in to the government.

The bills, however, would allow some purchases. The armed forces and the police, of course, could go on buying and using handguns. Importers, dealers, and antique gun collectors could also purchase once they were licensed by the government. The bills, recognizing that target shooting with pistols is a legitimate sport, would allow gun clubs to be formed; a sports shooter could have and use a handgun once he'd joined a club.

Under Representative Mikva's proposed bill, gun club members would be able to use their handguns only on the club premises. "This may be a slight inconvenience," he says, "to the relatively few people who like to shoot at targets in their backyards, but when measured against the lives that will be saved, this seems a small concession for sportsmen to make." The weapons would

(73)

never leave the club grounds and would be securely stored against theft.

Delegate Fauntroy's bill wants stiff penalties for violations of the ban. "The penalty for manufacturing, selling, or trading in handguns," he explains, "would be $5000 or imprisonment of not more than five years, or both." Anyone illegally owning a handgun could be fined $2000 and/or put in prison for up to two years.

In calling for currently owned handguns to be surrendered to the government, Representative Bingham's bill gives people 180 days to turn them in. Owners would receive a cash reimbursement for each handgun. Once the 180 days are up, owners could still turn in their guns without getting into trouble, but would not be reimbursed for them.

Representative Mikva would have the government pay a fair market price for each gun surrendered. Delegate Fauntroy suggests that each person receive "a tax credit equal to the fair market value of the gun or $25, whichever is greater."

On three counts, anti-control supporters oppose the surrender program idea. First, they contend that many law-abiding citizens will refuse to hand in their weapons; simply because they wish to go on protecting themselves and their families, they'll be turned into lawbreakers.

Second, the police will have to go hunting for the guns that are not surrendered. The hunt, with officers hammering on doors and confiscating the weapons they find, may well violate a citizen's constitutional safeguards against "search and seizure." The country could be well on its way to becoming a police state.

Finally, the anti-control group argues that the cost of paying for the surrendered handguns will be too much for the American taxpayer to bear. There are currently between 40 and 50 million handguns in the nation. If they're all turned in and if the average market value for

(74)

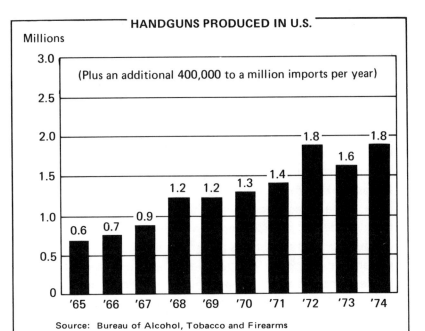

HANDGUNS PRODUCED IN U.S.

Millions

(Plus an additional 400,000 to a million imports per year)

Year	Millions
'65	0.6
'66	0.7
'67	0.9
'68	1.2
'69	1.2
'70	1.3
'71	1.4
'72	1.8
'73	1.6
'74	1.8

Source: Bureau of Alcohol, Tobacco and Firearms

U.S. VIOLENT CRIME—1975
(To nearest 1,000 crimes)

	All Weapons	Handguns (Est.)
Murder	21,000	11,000
Aggravated Assault	485,000	120,000
Robbery	465,000	150,000
Rape	56,000	(?)
Approximate Total	**1,000,000**	**300,000**

300,000 actual or potential HANDGUN deaths annually!

Source: House Judiciary Committee Report No. 94-1103

each is set somewhere between $25 and $75, the cost will run into the billions.

(*Author's note:* A program of surrendering guns for money was tried recently at the local level. The results were indecisive. In 1974, the people of Baltimore, Maryland, were asked to turn in their guns for $50 each. In a two-and-a-half-month period, 13,500 firearms were handed over and $660,000 was paid by the city for them. The program had to be stopped short because federal funds that were needed to keep it going failed to materialize. It had been hoped that the program would reduce the number of gun crimes in the city; instead, they went up during the time of the program. But many citizens and a number of police officials felt that the removal of all those guns would certainly help to reduce future violent crimes and senseless shootings in the city.)

Pro-control supporters answer the various anti-control arguments by pointing to the way Representative Bingham's bill protects the hesitant gun owner from criminal penalty when he turns his gun in late. They also say that educational programs could encourage owners to cooperate in the surrender. Owners could be urged to replace the dangerous handgun with some other form of protection — perhaps with a long gun, a burglar alarm, or triggered lights.

So far as the hunt for withheld guns is concerned, the problem here is the same as in the search for any illegal article. The rules governing "search and seizure" would have to be strictly followed by the police. Finally, the lives saved by the surrender program would be more than worth the monetary cost.

Limited Bans

Legislation against handguns of a small size has come mainly in proposals aimed at the Saturday Night Special.

In 1972, Senator Birch Bayh of Indiana authored a measure prohibiting the manufacture, importation, sale, and ownership of Specials. His bill roughly defined the Special as a handgun obviously not meant for or "readily adaptable" to sporting purposes. The measure passed the Senate 68 to 25. It did not, however, win in the House.

Three years later, Edward Levi, the attorney general under President Gerald R. Ford, came up with a similar proposal. Again, the "sporting purposes" definition was used. The proposal also called for a fourteen-day waiting period between the time a customer bought a handgun of any sort and the time he took it home. Authorities were to check the purchaser's background during the waiting period.

No congressional action was taken on the measure, in great part because it did not receive President Ford's wholehearted support. Mr. Ford, as he himself remarked during the 1976 presidential debates with Democratic candidate Jimmy Carter, favored strong and strictly enforced criminal laws rather than gun controls.

Also causing trouble for both the Bayh and Levi proposals was the fact that many legislators objected to the definition given the Special. Some thought it too vague and wanted a definition that spelled out size, quality of materials, and safety features.

Because of the difficulties involved in finding a satisfactory definition, legislators know that they may be a long while in coming up with a law restricting Specials. Many feel that, in the meantime, the Special can best be attacked by strengthening the Gun Control Act of 1968. In particular, they say, one glaring loophole in the act must be closed.

Thousands of handguns — many of them cheaply made — are manufactured abroad, and the act prohibits them from being imported into this country. But it does

(77)

not say that their *parts* cannot be imported. Foreign manu-facturers have sidestepped the act for years now simply by shipping in the parts and having the guns assembled here. Assembly plants in such states as Florida, Georgia, and Maryland put together some 772,000 foreign hand-guns a year for sale in the U.S.

Chapter Nine

AGAINST OWNERSHIP

Now let's turn to the opposite side of the coin. What could you as a legislator do to control the purchase and ownership of handguns?

Here are some avenues that you could take.

LIMITING PURCHASES

Today, an American can purchase as many handguns as he wants and as often as he wishes. Basically, all that the law demands is that he buy from a licensed seller. There's nothing to prevent him even from buying a freight car full of handguns. A multiple sale such as this, however, must be reported to the BATF by the dealer.

Obviously, the number of handguns that now reach the public would be quickly and significantly cut by a law that limits the purchases a citizen may make. Perhaps you'd allow him to buy one gun at a time at given intervals. Perhaps he could buy once a month. Perhaps once or twice a year.

RESTRICTIVE
LICENSING

Without mentioning the term itself, we've already talked about the process called *restrictive licensing*. It's contained in the Bingham, Mikva, and Fauntroy bills to ban handguns throughout the nation.

The bills, while keeping the handgun from the general public, would allow some purchases, restricting them to the armed forces, the police, security guards, dealers, collectors, and gun clubs. All these organizations and individuals would have to apply to the government for a license before a purchase could be made.

In the case of individual applicants, a thorough investigation into each purchaser's background and his reasons for wanting the handgun would be made before the license was granted. The armed forces and the police would be licensed as organizations and then would be responsible for arming their members and training them in the proper use of the gun.

Gun clubs would have to prove that their premises are suitable for target shooting and that the handguns would be kept safely stored against theft when not actually being used.

Though the Bingham, Mikva, and Fauntroy bills tie it in with a production ban, restrictive licensing could be tried by itself. But the two approaches might work best together, with the production ban cutting down on the flow of handguns while the licensing spells out those relatively few people able to purchase the ones that do become available.

Together — especially if strictly enforced and joined with a program of surrender to the government — they could make it exceedingly difficult for troublemakers to find a handgun anywhere.

(80)

NATIONAL
REGISTRATION

Let's say that you think every citizen has a right to own a firearm. But you'd still like some sort of control — one that would discourage criminals without depriving law-abiding Americans of their handguns. This might be accomplished by having everyone register his handguns with the federal government. Then, should any gun ever cause trouble, you'd be able to trace its owner.

Every present handgun owner would be asked to register his name and the serial number of his weapon. Whenever a new purchase was made, the dealer would register the buyer's name and the gun's serial number. Should friends swap guns, they would have to inform the government of the trade. All this information would be sent to a central agency in Washington, D.C., and stored in a computer.

Under present law, a customer's name and the serial number of the gun are recorded by the dealer at the time of purchase. But this information is filed by and at the dealer's place of business. The gun can then be traced within the state, but if the gun is used in a crime in some other state, the authorities in that state have little or no way of knowing where it came from. With a computer system in Washington, guns used in crimes anywhere in the country could be traced to their owners. Actually, a national tracing system of this type has already been started; it's the BATF's National Firearms Tracing Center, which has been at work in Washington since 1972.

Also, a national registration program would catch all those handguns that were purchased long ago, before the dealer had to report the buyer's name and the weapon's serial number.

If you wished, rather than having one agency in

Washington, you might set up computers in each of the states and tie them together for the exchange of information. Or you might combine the state systems with a federal one. Many pro-control advocates believe that a single federal computer will be best; it's easier to trace something from just one source than from fifty.

A registration program would do little to reduce crime and violence because it would do nothing to ban handguns. But, just as fingerprint files do, the computer could help to solve crimes by pinpointing the owner. Should a gun used in a crime prove to have been stolen from a law-abiding citizen, at least the police would learn something of its history and might have a clue as to where to start their investigation. And guns that have been simply lost could be returned to their owners when found.

Anti-control supporters are as opposed to registration as to the surrender program. They begin by arguing that the computer will be of little value in police investigations because criminals simply won't register their guns. Next, they estimate that the cost of processing the registrations for the 40 million or more handguns in the U.S. will run to a staggering $4 or $5 billion. The figure is based on a processing cost of about $100 a gun. Then, on top of the initial expense, taxpayers will have to meet the annual bill for processing new guns and maintaining the central computer agency.

REGIONAL CONTROL

Restrictive licensing and registration are both national controls. If you didn't wish to work on a country-wide scale, you might choose regional control instead.

Regional control would ban handguns to the general public only in certain areas. The areas would be those that have exceptionally high crime rates.

(82)

But how would you decide on the areas?

A continuing study that the government makes could be of help here. Called the *Standard Metropolitan Statistical Areas* (SMSAs), it keeps a running tally of the incidence of crime and violence in major cities, suburban areas, and selected rural areas. You could watch the SMSAs and call for regional control in any area where the crime rate climbs to 100 percent of the national rate.

A strict gun ban would immediately go into effect there. It would remain in force until the rate drops back to a certain point. The area could then elect to drop or continue the ban.

The system could also be set up so that areas with low crime rates could join in if they wished.

To be truly effective, regional control would need to be coupled to a program of national registration. Then the police would be better able to track down the owners of guns that are slipped into the controlled area from the outside.

Within the controlled area, certain people (police, dealers, and so on) would be allowed to purchase and own handguns. But they would first have to obtain a license or a "Federal Handgun Owners Identification Card." They could then only buy a handgun from a dealer licensed by the government.

Many legislators on both sides of the gun debate view regional control as a good and practical approach.

One fact makes their feelings easily understood: The two camps in the debate have generally been divided along geographic lines. Legislators who represent urban areas where crime is commonplace favor gun control because their constituents are in need of protection. But legislators from rural areas usually oppose control; their constitutents see little crime and look on any control as a threat to their hunting and sporting activities. Regional control, then, could serve as a neat compromise, banning the handgun where a ban is most needed, but leaving guns alone in those areas where a ban is unnecessary.

PERMISSIVE LICENSING

This approach is similar to the control laws that are now on the federal books. It would permit all law-abiding citizens to buy firearms. But it would prohibit those people who are presently not allowed to own guns — felons, mental incompetents, minors, and the like — from purchasing any of these weapons.

There would, however, be some major differences. All handgun owners (and perhaps long gun owners, too) would be required to obtain a license. This is something that federal law does not demand today. At present — as charted in chapter three — only certain states require licenses.

Also required would be a waiting period of several days between the time a gun was bought and then taken home. Current federal law doesn't provide for such a delay, and by the close of the 1970s, only thirteen states carried this provision on their books. The delay would give authorities time to check the purchaser's background and could serve as a "cooling off" period for someone buying a gun in anger. As we'll find in the next chapter, Washington has seen two proposals that call for a substantial delay. One asked for a fourteen-day wait. The other seeks a twenty-one-day delay.

Permissive licensing would overcome a very serious problem of today. As federal law now stands, a dealer has no way of knowing whether he is selling a gun to a customer who is forbidden from owning one. The only way a dealer knows if he is selling to a person allowed to own a gun is if he is personally acquainted with the buyer or has heard something about the buyer's background. The dealer is protected against this difficulty only in those states and local areas that have "waiting period" laws. The delay-after-purchase would enable the authorities to weed out anyone on the forbidden list. If the delay was demanded by federal law, the background check on the customer could be made by both local police and the FBI.

Under permissive licensing, you might require a citizen to take a gun test similar to the one for obtaining a driver's license. The buyer might have to answer questions on gun regulations and then demonstrate that he knows how to handle the weapon safely. You might also call for the gun buyer to attend and pass police-approved or police-conducted safety courses. And you might insist that he carry theft and liability insurance on his firearms.

Pro-control supporters look on permissive licensing with mixed feelings. Some like the idea of testing and licensing gun owners in the same manner as motorists. It's an acknowledged fact that an automobile is a deadly weapon and that every effort must be made to place it only in capable hands. The same should apply to the gun. If a person is going to own a firearm, then the wisest course is to see that he is qualified properly and trained to use it.

But, on the other hand, many pro-control supporters point to a problem with the automobile. Licensing and training requirements have not kept the automobile out of careless or reckless hands. The car kills thousands of people annually and injures several million others. There may be no reason to assume that if the gun were similarly licensed it would kill or injure fewer people than it does today.

Finally, pro-control supporters do not look favorably on permissive licensing because it would not cut down on the number of handguns in the nation and would allow millions more to be purchased in the years to come. It would, they agree, help to keep handguns from those on the forbidden list, but these people would simply turn to other sources for their purchases. As a result, they feel, a vast black market in guns would develop. Worst of all, as one pro-control group puts it, the system would "officially legalize and perpetuate an armed American society."

LEGISLATION ON OWNERSHIP

In the late 1970s, various laws dealing with handgun ownership were proposed by legislators on both sides of the control debate.

Senator Edward Kennedy of Massachusetts, Representative Ronald Dellums of California, Representative Gilbert Gude of Maryland, and Representative Robert McClory of Illinois all asked for laws requiring handgun licensing and registration.

Their bills varied in content. Some wanted to see not just handguns but all firearms registered. Some wanted all gun owners to be licensed. Others, working along the lines described in chapter eight, were interested only in licensing people in the firearms business.

Senator Jacob Javits of New York authored a bill calling for regional control.

Many legislators advised that the nation's crime and violence could best be reduced by stiffening the penalties listed in the 1968 Gun Control Act or by adding new penalties for crimes involving the gun.

At the end of the 1970s there were some thirty-nine bills pending in Congress — thirty-five in the House and four in the Senate — that would make it a federal crime to violate any state law involving the use of firearms. This would open the way for federal authorities to join with state and local officials in investigating and prosecuting a gun crime.

The gun control debate — and the search for an answer to it — entered the 1980s.

Chapter Ten

WHERE DO WE STAND NOW?

In the preceding nine chapters, we've looked at all sides of the gun-control problem and at what can be done to solve it to one degree or another. Now a new question must be asked: Where does the United States presently stand on the road to a solution?

WASHINGTON IN SEARCH OF A SOLUTION

The nation's capital took four steps in search of a solution in the mid to late 1970s. The first step began in 1975 when a subcommittee launched a study of the various control bills that had been proposed by members of the House of Representatives. The subcommittee was headed by Representative John Conyers of Michigan. The job of the subcommittee was to select those bills that it thought should be sent to the House floor for a vote. If it wished, the subcommittee could shape them into a single bill that could go in their place.

On the basis of the study, Representative Conyers developed a bill and presented it to the subcommittee. His bill contained three points: (1) it banned all easily conceal-able handguns; (2) it increased the licensing fee for dealers, in an effort to cut their number from 150,000 to around 40,000; and (3) it called for the establishment of a federal agency to trace handguns that had been used in crimes. This tracing agency would be established instead of a national registration program, and it would work with local authorities in tracing the handguns.

The subcommittee membership, which was made up of legislators on both sides of the gun-control debate, could not agree on the Conyers bill. But they worked out a com-promise measure over a period of weeks. In April 1976, they sent it to the House for consideration.

The compromise did anything but make pro-control supporters happy. Rather than banning all easily conceal-able handguns, it hit only at Saturday Night Specials, pro-hibiting their manufacture and sale. Worse yet, all the pro-hibitions were for the *future*; the ownership and sale of Specials already on the market were to be permitted. Next, dealer fees were increased just slightly. Finally, the com-promise made no mention at all of a national tracing agency.

Pro-control representatives were so disappointed that many said they would not vote for the bill. Then word reached the House that even if the bill was passed, it would be ignored when it arrived in the Senate for a vote. The senators had no wish to handle as controversial an issue as gun control during a presidential election year. The result: the bill fell by the wayside.

The second step came when Jimmy Carter entered the White House. While campaigning for the presidency in 1976, Mr. Carter argued in favor of controls that would keep the handgun out of criminal reach. He also spoke in favor of some kind of limited handgun registration. He added that, as a longtime hunter, he had no wish to see controls enacted against the rifle and the shotgun.

(88)

Soon after taking office, Mr. Carter asked the Department of Justice to work out a handgun-control proposal for his consideration.

The proposal that took shape was similar to the Conyers bill. It sought to ban the easily concealable handgun. Further, it advised that there should be a limit to the number of legal-sized handguns that a customer could purchase; a figure of one purchase per month was suggested. And the proposal recommended that there be a waiting period of fourteen days between the time of the purchase and the time that the gun would be taken home.

A major section of the proposal called for the strengthening of the Gun Control Act of 1968 so that certain loopholes in it would be closed. The loophole most in need of closing was the one that prohibited the import of cheap handguns, but allowed their parts to be shipped in for assembly here. A gun-assembly business had flourished in the southern part of the nation in recent years. One main center for assembly was Miami, Florida.

Though President Carter spoke in favor of handgun registration during the 1976 campaign, the proposal made no mention of registration or a national tracing agency. Rather, it asked for stringent dealer controls, such as the filing of purchase information with the police. These controls would make it easier for local authorities to trace a gun from a seller to a purchaser. The proposal also recommended a substantial increase in dealer and manufacturing license fees.

Why was neither registration nor a national tracing agency mentioned? Both would require the creation of new federal bureaus. Mr. Carter was against the formation of expensive new agencies. Rather, he wanted to see the number already in Washington decreased.

Finally, the proposal advised that the Justice Department join with the BATF in managing any new control law. The BATF, as it had been doing under the 1968 Gun Control Act, would enforce the new legislation. The Justice Department would administer the legislation. It would also set policy as to the particular types of handguns affected by the legislation.

Nothing came of the proposal during Mr. Carter's four years in the White House. Gun control had to take a back seat to other matters that plagued the Carter presidency, for example, the energy crisis, the sagging economy, and the Americans held hostage for more than a year in Iran. The proposal died when Mr. Carter was defeated by Ronald Reagan in the 1980 presidential election.

Although gun control had to take a back seat during the Carter administration, there was still some action on it. The third of the four steps came late in Mr. Carter's term. Two anti-control legislators — Republican Senator James A. McClure of Idaho and Democratic Representative Harold L. Volkmer of Missouri — proposed a bill for the Senate and the House in 1979.

The bill was intended to amend the 1968 Gun Control Act. It permitted anyone to buy a gun in any state as long as the laws of the state where the purchase was made and the laws of the buyer's home state were not violated in any way. Additionally, the checks on the buyer that were presently required in his home state and in the state of purchase would be continued.

Additionally, the bill sought to ease the Gun Control Act's restrictions on the transportation of guns between states. The measure also required that federal agents show reasonable cause before inspecting a dealer's records for accuracy.

Soon after the bill was written, it was reported that 102 representatives and 44 senators supported it. Various reasons were given for the support, beginning with the basic feeling that law-abiding Americans have the right to own a gun for legal purposes. Some of the supporting legislators liked the measure because it placed gun control principally in state and local hands; many disliked the 1968 Gun Control Act because they felt it prompted too much interference in citizen affairs by the federal government. Others felt that the provisions of the 1968 Act were too stringent on legitimate gun owners. And still others felt that something had to be done to curtail the power of the BATF; they accused the agency of constantly trying to obtain heavier gun controls without first going to Congress for action.

As this chapter is being written, the McClure-Volkmer bill is still under study in Congress.

The fourth and final step was taken in 1979 by Senator Edward Kennedy and Democratic Representative Peter Rodino of New Jersey. Like Volkmer and McClure, they authored a bill to amend the Gun Control Act. Their bill, however, called for stricter controls than those found in the Act.

The measure never came up for a vote in Congress and was eventually set aside. But the murder of singer John Lennon and the attempted assassination of President Ronald Reagan have returned it to the forefront. The Kennedy-Rodino bill has been reintroduced and is about to come under serious study by Congress. Because of this anticipated study, we will discuss the bill more fully.

But, first, we need to pause and look at another recent development — the views on gun control that Ronald Reagan brought with him to the White House. They are views that differ from President Carter's. They may have a strong effect on how Congress will act on the Kennedy-Rodino bill or on any other control measure.

PRESIDENT REAGAN
AND GUN CONTROL

Gun-control advocates felt that they might be facing a difficult period as the 1980s dawned. Not only had gun control taken a back seat during the Carter years, but now it also seemed to be fading from the public's mind as a welter of other problems closed in on the nation. Finally, the newly elected President was not a strong pro-control man. Mr. Reagan's stand on the issue was identical to the one taken by all anti-control supporters; he argued that the fight should be against the criminal who uses the gun rather than the gun itself.

In an interview printed in *Field and Stream* magazine during the 1980 presidential race, Mr. Reagan made his views clear. He said that the weapon itself was not the problem. After all, a rock could be a weapon. What mattered was a criminal's use of the weapon.

While campaigning for the presidency, Mr. Reagan stated his opinions on gun control in a number of speeches. He told his listeners that controls would interfere with the rights of law-abiding citizens to purchase and own firearms for legal purposes, but wouldn't be able to do a thing to stop criminals from obtaining guns by illegal means. He expanded on this point in the *Field and Stream* interview by saying that any criminal could put together a home-made gun — a "zip" gun — with a piece of pipe. Only a few hours work would be required to do the job.

Mr. Reagan also spoke out against gun registration during the campaign. He argued that registration "has always been an aid to totalitarian takeovers in other countries." By pinpointing the ownership and the location of millions of weapons, registration would make it easy for an oppressive government to move in and take them over. The people would then be left helpless. The people must always be able to defend themselves against a would-be dictator, he stated.

Mr. Reagan favored the kind of law that had been enacted in California while he was Governor there. Aimed at the criminal rather than the gun, it called for extra prison time to be given to anyone who committed a crime while having a gun in his or her possession. It did not matter whether the gun was actually used or not; an added term of five to fifteen years was to be imposed. When the law was first passed, judges had the option of granting probation in place of the additional time. Later, that option was removed. The extra prison time was made mandatory.

In his *Field and Stream* interview, Mr. Reagan recounted that while serving as Governor of California he had received a letter from a former inmate at San Quentin Prison, which is located just north of San Francisco. The man wrote to say that it would mean a great deal to criminals if guns were banned to the general public. It would remove, he wrote, a great hazard to his profession. Criminals could then break into a home or store without the fear of coming face-to-face with an armed owner. The situation would be "heaven," the man added.

These, then, were Mr. Reagan's views on gun control when he won the presidential election in November 1980. He had held them for years, as any study of his many speeches and magazine articles reveal. And he did not change them in the dark days that were to come — days that would see him struck and wounded by a would-be assassin's bullet.

THE DARK DAYS OF
DECEMBER AND MARCH

The year 1980 ended in tragic bursts of gunfire. There were more shots on March 30, 1981. These new outbreaks of violence stunned not only the nation but the world.

December 5, 1980
Dr. Michael Halberstam was a highly respected physician in Washington, D.C., and the editor of *Modern Medicine* magazine. On December 5, 1980, Dr. Halberstam surprised a burglar in his home. The intruder drew a gun, shot the doctor, and fled into the night. Badly wounded and bleed-

ing, Dr. Halberstam gave chase in his car. He succeeded in running the man down before he himself died. Dr. Halberstam was forty-eight years old at the time of his death.

December 8, 1980

Tragedy struck again on December 8 — just three days later — when singer John Lennon and his wife, Yoko Ono, were returning home after an evening out. Lennon was known the world over. He had first come to fame as a member of the Beatles and then had gone on to win honors on his own as a composer and solo vocalist.

The couple crossed the courtyard in front of their New York City apartment building. A young man in a dark overcoat stepped from the shadows behind them. He called, "Mr. Lennon." As Lennon turned, the young man pointed a small revolver at the singer and fired at least four shots. Yoko Ono was not struck. But her husband staggered and fell to the pavement with a bullet in his chest. John Lennon was dead at age forty.

Police arrested the young killer at the scene. He was twenty-five years old and his name was Mark David Chapman. A native of Georgia, he had suffered a long history of mental instability. In earlier years, he had twice tried to commit suicide. He had been placed in a mental institution at one time, but he had been released. The police discovered an autograph album in his pocket. In it was Lennon's signature. The singer had given Chapman his autograph just a few hours before the shooting.

March 30, 1981

The early afternoon hours of Monday, March 30, 1981, found President Reagan at the Washington Hilton Hotel, a five-minute drive from the White House. He was there to deliver a short speech to the 3,500 delegates attending an

(94)

AFL-CIO convention. The President completed his speech a few minutes before 2:30 P.M. He and his aides prepared to leave the hotel via a side entrance reserved for important visitors. The President's limousine was parked at the head of a line of cars at the curb.

Clustered near the entrance were reporters, police, and passers-by. They were assembled behind a red-velvet rope that extended across the sidewalk and was meant to keep them safely distant from the President. Standing in the midst of the waiting group was a twenty-five-year-old man. His name was John W. Hinckley. A .22-caliber Roehm RG14 revolver lay concealed in his coat pocket. The parts of the gun had been manufactured in West Germany. They had been shipped to Miami for assembly. The gun usually retailed for about $47.50. Hinckley had bought it some months earlier — along with an identical weapon — in Dallas, Texas.

Hinckley was the son of a wealthy and respected Denver family. Though well educated, he had spent the last few years as a drifter, wandering from one job to another. He was known among his friends for his violent political views. Hinckley had once been a member of the American Nazi Party but had been dropped because his ideas were too harsh even for these supporters of the principles of German dictator Adolf Hitler.

There could be no doubt that Hinckley was as emotionally unstable as John Lennon's killer. On seeing the motion picture *Taxi Driver* (which dealt with the plans to kill a United States senator), he had fallen in love with one of its stars, eighteen-year-old Jodie Foster. Miss Foster, now a student at Yale University in New Haven, Connecticut, seems not to have known Hinckley. However, he had sent her fan letters at one time and had recently slipped several notes, signed "John," under the door of her room at school. She would be shocked to learn that he had written her a love letter just the night before. In it, he spoke of what he planned to do that day — kill the President of the United States.

At 2:25 P.M., Mr. Reagan's assistants began to emerge from the hotel. Among the first to leave were two of his closest aides. One was his Press Secretary, James Brady. The other was Michael Deaver, Deputy White House Chief of Staff. They headed for the line of cars parked at the curb. Their destination was the vehicle just behind Mr. Reagan's limousine. Their route put them between Hinckley and the limousine. Standing nearby as they hurried past was Washington police officer Thomas Delahanty.

Seconds later, Mr. Reagan appeared. He had to walk 25 feet (7.7 m) to reach his limousine. Behind him came Secret Service agent Jerry Parr. Another agent, Timothy McCarthy, was walking close to the President. A reporter in the crowd called to the President, hoping to attract his attention for a question. Mr. Reagan smiled and raised his arm to wave.

In the instant that President Reagan waved, Hinckley acted. The would-be assassin pulled the revolver from his pocket. He dropped to one knee. Holding the gun in both hands, he took aim and began firing. The shots had a light, rattling sound to them, like firecrackers bursting. In two seconds, Hinckley emptied the gun of its six bullets.

Terror flashed along the sidewalk. One bullet whistled past Michael Deaver's ear, missing him by scant inches. Press Secretary James Brady pitched forward with a bullet in his brain. Police officer Thomas Delahanty spun and fell; he had been struck in the neck. At the sound of the shots, Secret Service agent Timothy McCarthy turned in the direction of the perpetrator, putting himself between Hinckley and Mr. Reagan. McCarthy went up on tiptoes, doubled over, and then fell. A bullet had hit him just below the chest.

The gunshots startled Mr. Reagan. A reporter later said that he saw the President turn pale. Mr. Reagan paused at the open door of his limousine — but for no more than a split-second. Then Secret Service agent Jerry Parr grabbed him from behind. Parr doubled the President over to reduce his size as a target and pushed him into the limousine. The agent plunged in after him. The door slammed. The limousine sped away. On the sidewalk, there was now pandemonium. Some reporters, police, and government agents swarmed over Hinckley, while others began to tend the wounded.

The presidential limousine headed for the White House. At first, Mr. Reagan felt no pain. He was sure that he hadn't been hit. Then he began to complain of having difficulty with his breathing. Agent Parr thought that Mr. Reagan might have broken a rib in the dive into the car. Parr ordered the chauffeur to drive to George Washington University Hospital.

It was then learned that Mr. Reagan had indeed been hit. One of Hinckley's bullets had struck the side of the limousine. Ricocheting, the slug had entered the President's left side, just below the armpit. It had traveled down his side, caromed off a rib, and punctured his left lung, coming to rest at last just 3 inches (7.6 cm) from his heart.

Mr. Reagan underwent surgery to remove the bullet. Four hours after the shooting, he was in the recovery room. His next weeks were spent regaining his strength. He made a fine recovery and returned to his duties in the White House.

Miraculously, there were no deaths in the shooting. Secret Service agent McCarthy and police officer Delahanty underwent surgery and recovered. The most seriously wounded of the victims was Press Secretary Brady. He was so badly injured that within hours after the shooting the report that he had died was flashed across the nation. But he courageously clung to life throughout the next days and, after surgery, began a slow recovery. At present, he is continuing to recuperate.

The Aftermath

The assassination attempt on the President and the deaths of John Lennon and Dr. Halberstam catapulted the gun-control issue from the back seat position that it had occupied for months. The shootings, reminding everyone anew of the violence so rampant in the country, unleashed a fresh wave of public outrage and concern. Magazine articles and newspaper editorials attacked our widespread use of firearms. The nation's legislators — depending on where they stood in the gun-control debate — began to think again of measures to regulate the gun itself or to impose harsher penalties on those who misused it. Some legislators took a new look at the many bills that had been proposed in Congress over the recent years. Some planned to introduce measures of their own.

Of all the possible measures, two seem due to receive the most attention in Congress — the McClure-Volkmer bill and the Kennedy-Rodino bill. We have already looked at the provisions in the McClure-Volkmer measure. Now let's turn to the bill authored by Senator Edward Kennedy and Representative Peter Rodino.

THE KENNEDY-RODINO BILL

The Kennedy-Rodino measure is aimed exclusively at the handgun. It is similar to much of the legislation proposed over the past years, in that it does not contain provisions about the rifle and the shotgun. This is because it considers the rifle and the shotgun as weapons used mainly for hunting and target shooting purposes. The current measure is entitled The Handgun Crime Control Bill.

The bill contains six major provisions. First, it requires that a mandatory prison sentence be imposed on anyone who uses a handgun in the commission of a felony. The prison sentence is lighter than the one required by Califor-

(98)

nia law. A two-year term is to be given for a first offense. Each subsequent offense is to bring five years. The California law, you'll remember, calls for a term of five to fifteen years.

Next, the bill requires a prison sentence for anyone who is found carrying a handgun without a permit. This provision is similar to a law currently on the books in several states. The best known of these laws is in Massachusetts. Enacted in 1974, the Massachusetts law carries a one-year prison term for anyone found guilty of carrying an unlicensed handgun. The Kennedy-Rodino bill also calls for a one-year sentence.

Third, the bill requires that a buyer must wait twenty-one days (as opposed to fourteen days in the Carter proposal) before being allowed to take the gun home. During that time, a check would be made on the buyer's background to ascertain if he is fit for ownership. The check would attempt to make sure that the purchaser is not a felon, a drug addict, a minor, or someone with a history of mental disorders. The check would be made by local police and the FBI.

Fourth, the bill bans the manufacture, the assembly, and the sale of all handguns classed as Saturday Night Specials.

Senator Kennedy and Representative Rodino have not attempted to define exactly the kinds of guns that can be called Saturday Night Specials. Rather, they ask that present and future handguns be established as Specials on the basis of several factors, among them the cheapness of manufacture and the ease with which the weapons could be concealed. The guns would also be judged on whether they were suitable for such legitimate activities as hunting and target shooting or whether their main purpose seemed to be to inflict injury. A special commission would be formed to decide which handguns, now and in the future, fit the description of a Special. Handguns not meeting the description could be legally manufactured and sold.

Finally, the bill places certain demands on owners, manufacturers, and dealers. Owners, for instance, would be required to report all thefts of their weapons to the police. Manufacturers would have to keep closer tabs on the distribution of their products than is presently required. Pawnshops would no longer be able to secure licenses as gun dealerships. Studies have shown that some 35 percent of the guns used in crimes are obtained from pawnshops.

The Kennedy-Rodino bill is causing much controversy among legislators and the public at large. Anti-control supporters regard it in the same way that they have regarded previous control measures — as a bill that jeopardizes the rights of Americans to own firearms, that opens the way to stricter controls and further government intervention in private affairs, and that fails to attack the real problem — the criminal. Pro-control forces see it in exactly the opposite light. To them, it is at least an initial move against both the handgun and the criminal.

Among the greatest supporters of the bill is Handgun Control, Inc., an organization that we mentioned earlier in this book under its original name, the National Council to Control Handguns (see pages 42 and 48–49). The organization, which lobbies in the nation's capital for strong control laws, recently adopted its new name.

The Handgun Control vice president is Charles Orasin. In a 1981 interview for *America* magazine, Mr. Orasin told Jesuit writer George Anderson that the whole point of the bill is to make it more difficult for criminals to secure pistols and revolvers. He argued that gun control laws are, at base, anti-crime laws and not regulations to keep citizens from obtaining firearms for legitimate purposes. Nor are they intended to take firearms away from people properly licensed to own them.

A number of observers across the country — observers on both sides of the debate — see several possible flaws in the Kennedy-Rodino bill, however. In the minds of many, one major shortcoming is a provision that allows a customer to buy two legally-manufactured guns a year. Obviously, the provision tries to strike a middle ground between unlimited ownership and an outright ban.

But it has brought a cry of consternation from several quarters, including the *Nation* magazine. In a 1981 issue, the magazine suggested that the two-a-year limit is really no limit at all. The *Nation* went on to say that statistics show that there are presently some 56 million gun owners in the country. A percentage of them — say, 10 percent or 5.6 million — would probably see the limitation as a sign of tougher controls to come. They might then rush out and stock up on two guns a year as a hedge against the future. If so, this would mean an annual sale of about 11 million handguns — far more than the 2 million now being sold. The bill, then, would not help matters. It would worsen them.

The *Nation* article touched on another point that bothers many people — the ban on Saturday Night Specials. The feeling here is that, on two counts, there should be a move to ban all handguns. First, if the ban is limited only to the Special, any manufacturer will be able to alter the design of his product (perhaps increasing the size or upgrading the materials slightly) so that it manages to avoid being classed as a Special. The type of gun used in so many crimes would still be readily available for purchase.

Second, as the *Nation* points out, it must be remembered that, because of their shoddy construction, Saturday Night Specials often don't work well for the criminal. They often misfire. They are often inaccurate. They are flimsy and they break easily when dropped. If they alone are banned from the marketplace, the criminal will be able, by spending a few dollars more, to buy the more expensive and more accurate guns that are left. The results could be more deadly than those that have already been seen. The only answer, the pro-control advocates argue, is to ban all handguns, regardless of their quality.

Anti-control supporters are also speaking out against the ban of Specials, but for a different reason. They don't like the idea of a commission that would decide which present and future handguns would be classed as Specials. They argue that it would be easy for such a commission, if its membership is pro-control, to set definitions for the Special that will extend to even the best manufactured handguns. In effect, the commission could impose a total handgun ban on the nation.

As this chapter is being written, both the Kennedy-Rodino and the McClure-Volkmer bills are awaiting congressional study. The study should come in the near future — a near future that is clouded with many a question mark. Will the pro- and anti-control forces, as sharply divided as they are, be able to decide on one bill or another — or on any other proposal that comes to their attention? Or will they be able to come up with a workable compromise measure? And what influence will President Reagan's anti-control views — views that remain unchanged in the wake of that terrible March afternoon — have on the outcome?

These are questions that have no answers at present. Only time can provide the answers.

WHERE THE PUBLIC STANDS

Thus far in this chapter, by looking at the various congressional measures that have been proposed in the late 1970s and early 1980s, we've seen where Washington stands in its search for a solution to the gun control problem. But what about the American public? Where do we stand on the issue? What kind of control laws do we want? Will we be content with the Kennedy-Rodino bill or the McClure-Volkmer bill should one of them be enacted? Or will we want something more strict? Or something more lenient?

Recent public opinion polls can give us a clue. They were taken by the George Gallup Organization, Louis Harris and Associates, and CBS News. They asked Americans what they thought about the three main types of control that have been discussed in this book — national registration, regional handgun control, and a nationwide ban on handguns.

In addition, the Gallup Organization and the Decision Making Information company have asked Americans what they believe to be the major causes of crime in the nation.

Let's see what the public said.

Registration
In 1967 and again in 1975, the Louis Harris pollsters asked a number of Americans: "Would you favor federal laws which would control the sale of handguns, such as making all persons register all gun purchases no matter where the purchases were made?

The question got the following results in 1967: 66 percent in favor; 28 percent against. By 1975, the margin had widened. Now 73 percent favored registration at the time of purchase. The opposition had dropped to 24 percent.

In 1975, Harris pollsters also asked who would favor or oppose registering every handgun owned in the nation. CBS News wanted to know the same thing. And Gallup went a step farther and asked how Americans felt about registering *all* types of firearms.

Everyone came up with markedly similar results. Seventy-seven percent of the people questioned told the Harris pollsters that they were for total handgun registration; 19 percent were opposed. CBS found 78 percent for, and 20 percent against.

As for the registration of all firearms, Gallup reported that opinion ran 67 percent in favor and 27 percent against. Though the margin here was wide, it was slightly narrower than in 1974 when the same question was asked. At that time, 71 percent had been in favor, and 22 percent opposed.

Regional Control

In 1975 Harris found that public opinion was fairly evenly split on the idea of banning private citizens from owning handguns in high crime areas. Forty-four percent were for the ban. Forty-nine percent opposed it.

A Ban on Handguns

Public opinion was also very closely divided when, in 1975, the three companies asked how people felt about banning the private ownership of handguns throughout the nation. In the CBS poll, the opposition lost by a narrow margin. In the Harris and Gallup polls, it won.

The CBS findings: 51 percent in favor of the idea; 45 percent against.

The Harris findings: 57 percent opposed; 37 percent in favor.

The Gallup findings: 57 percent against; 41 percent for.

The Gallup Organization broke its nationwide findings down according to geographic area. Only in the eastern section of the country did those favoring a ban outnumber those opposed to a ban.

	For a Ban	Against a Ban	No Opinion
East	58%	37%	5%
Midwest	44%	53%	3%
South	27%	69%	4%
West	29%	65%	6%

The Cause Of Crime

Writing in a recent issue of *Field and Stream* magazine, columnist E. B. Mann reported that the National Rifle Association had hired the Decision Making Information company to do a public survey in 1978. DMI was to approach a number of people with the question: "According to national statistics, there has been a sharp increase in crime since 1963. In your own words, what would you say is the reason for the increase?"

Columnist Mann went on to report that the Gallup Organization had asked a similar question in a 1979 poll of its own. The Gallup pollsters inquired: "The federal government recently reported that there has been an increase in the national crime rate. What do you think is responsible for the increase?"

Mr. Mann then listed the opinions that were given. To begin, DMI reported that 52 percent of the people questioned felt that crime today was principally caused by social problems, such as a lack of respect for authority, a decaying morality, a permissive society, drug abuse, and the lack of parental discipline. Forty-two percent of the people questioned in the Gallup poll gave the same reasons.

Next, DMI reported that 40 percent of those interviewed blamed the high crime rate on the courts and the police. They felt that the courts were too lenient in their dealings with offenders. And they believed that police protection was inadequate or that the police were hampered in their duties by too many regulations. In the Gallup poll, 33 percent of the people came up with these same reasons.

Finally, Mr. Mann wrote, DMI reported that 29 percent of the pollees blamed inflation and the high cost of living for the increasing crime rate. Thirty-nine percent of the people questioned by Gallup felt the same way.

Mr. Mann remarked that the results of the two polls, though varying somewhat in their percentages, were remarkably alike. He then made the point that in both polls not even 1 percent of the people blamed guns for crime. Nor did they mention gun control as a possible solution for today's crime problem.

He then criticized the earlier polls. He said that by the very nature of their questions, they had been slanted in favor of pro-control answers. The questions, he said, had linked the crime rate to guns in the minds of the people being polled. The result had been a large number of pro-control answers. But, when the DMI and Gallup pollees had been given unbiased questions, the vast majority of the people had neither mentioned the gun itself as a cause of crime nor had regarded gun controls as a solution to crime.

All the above samplings of public opinion point up the dilemma that national legislators must face when they think about gun control. No matter how they move, they're sure to endanger their jobs by angering some of their constituents. Though some polls show that a majority of Americans would favor a registration program, there is a sizable segment of the public that would object most strenuously. As for regional control or a national handgun ban, the polls suggest that public opinion is still too closely divided for the legislators to want to take action. And what about the two polls that indicate that less than 1 percent of the people blame the gun for crime or see controls as a way to prevent it?

It might be said that our senators and representatives should move in a direction that they believe to be right, regardless of what the voters think. Undoubtedly, a number of them are doing so or will do so. But it also must be remembered that all legislators are in Washington to represent the views and desires of their constituents and not just their own commitments.

And so an exceedingly strong gun law at the national level — whether it be the Kennedy-Rodino bill or some other measure — promises to be a long time in coming, if it is to come at all. Should it be enacted, it will be after one of the most protracted and searching debates in the history of our country.

In the meantime, state and local areas will need to cope with the gun problem as they think best. This is happening right now. In areas hit by increasing crime and violence, strong laws are being passed or urged. As mentioned earlier, Massachusetts now has a law calling for anyone found carrying a firearm without proper authorization to be given a one-year prison sentence. New York has adopted the same law.

Washington, D.C., has made it almost impossible for anyone to obtain a handgun unless he is a law-enforcement officer, a security guard, or a courier. In San Francisco, the City Board of Appeals recently decided not to renew the permits that dealers need to sell handguns. Georgia has passed a law requiring a thirty-day wait before a customer can obtain a permit to buy a gun. Massachusetts, New York, and New Jersey require that thorough background checks be made on a customer before he is permitted to buy a gun.

In mid-1981, the city of Morton Grove, Illinois, (a suburb of Chicago) enacted an ordinance prohibiting the sale to and the possession of handguns by the general public. Exempted from the ordinance are police, security, and military personnel, plus licensed gun collectors. Mayor Jane Byrne of Chicago has expressed an interest in the ordinance and is looking into it for possible adoption.

These are just a few examples of what is happening across the country at the state and local level. On the other hand, little is being done — or perhaps needs to be done — in those rural and small-town areas that are rarely troubled by crime and violence. There, the belief that the private ownership of the gun is an American right and that the gun itself is a legitimate tool for sport and self-protection is being preserved and protected.

But, sooner or later, the whole issue must be resolved at the federal level, either with strong gun controls or a vigorous move against the nation's criminal element — or both.

Citizens can help resolve the issue by first coming to their own conclusions on what must be done. Then they can alert their friends to the problem, support those organizations favoring their views, and inform their local, state, and national representatives on where they stand.

Hopefully, all that you've read in this book will help you to answer that most important of questions:

Where do I stand?

Selected
Reading List

Those interested in studying further the gun-control debate will find the following materials to be of particular help:

BOOKS

Bloomgarden, Henry S. *The Gun: A Biography of the Gun That Killed John F. Kennedy*. New York: Grossman, 1975.

Bureau of Alcohol, Tobacco and Firearms. *Your 1977 Guide to Firearms Regulations*. Washington, D.C.: Government Printing Office.

Kukla, Robert J. *Gun Control: A Written Record of Efforts to Eliminate the Private Possession of Firearms in America*. Harrisburg, Pa.: Stackpole, 1973.

BOOKLETS

Firearms Prohibition — National Shooting Sports Foundation, 1075 Post Road, Riverdale, Conn. 06878

Gun Registration: Costly Experiment or Crime Cure? — National Shooting Sports Foundation, 1075 Post Road, Riverdale, Conn. 06878

Handgun Control: Issues and Alternatives — United States Conference of Mayors, 1620 Eye Street, N.W., Washington, D.C. 20006 (Cost: $5)

How Well Does the Handgun Protect You and Your Family? — United States Conference of Mayors, 1620 Eye Street, N.W., Washington, D.C. 20006 (Cost: $2)

The Case To Control Handguns — The National Council To Control Handguns, 810 18th Street, N.W., Washington, D.C. 20006

ARTICLES

Anderson, George M. "Those Uncontrollable Handguns." *America*, January 17, 1981.

Berg, David. "The Right to Bear Arms." *Newsweek*, December 29, 1980.

Caplan, David I. "Restoring the Balance: The Second Amendment Revisited." *The Fordham Urban Law Journal*, Fall 1976.

"Controversy over Proposed Federal Handgun Controls," *The Congressional Digest*. December 1975.

"Equal Protection," *The Nation*. May 16, 1981.

Goldwater, Barry. "Why Gun-Control Laws Don't Work." *Reader's Digest*, December 1975.

"Gun Law Versus Crime" (an interview with Senator Edward M. Kennedy and Don B. Kates). *Field & Stream*, August 1980.

Kates, Don B. "Gun Control: Can it Work?" *National Review*, May 15, 1981.

"The Last Day in the Life of John Lennon," *Time*. December 22, 1980.

Mann, E.B. "Gun-Ownership Views" (under his column "Our Endangered Tradition"). *Field & Stream*, July 1980.

"The Menace of any Shadow," *Time*. December 22, 1980.

Norman, Michael. "Gun Control." *New York Times Magazine*, May 3, 1981.

"Pro and Con: Should Handguns be Outlawed?" *U.S. News & World Report*. December 22, 1980.

Samson, Jack. "Ronald Reagan's Views on Guns, Hunting and Conservation." *Field & Stream*, October 1980.

"The Shooting of the President," *Newsweek*. April 13, 1981.

Smith, Adam. "Fifty Million Handguns: Does Violence have to be as American as Apple Pie?" *Esquire*, April 1981.

"Surge in Murders, Search for Solutions," *U.S. News & World Report*. December 22, 1980.

Index